"'We talk about community but not friendship.' Drew Hunter is right, and in *Made for Friendship* he fills the church's gap with deep theological truths and helpful practical tools regarding friendship. I'm grateful for this resource!"

Christine Hoover, author, *Messy Beautiful Friendship* and *Searching for Spring*

"Drew Hunter will capture you with his compelling vision of friendship. Beautifully written, these pages are filled with fresh insight and practical wisdom. Reading this book will ignite your desire to be a better friend and to savor the joys of friendship."

Colin S. Smith, Senior Pastor, The Orchard, Arlington Heights, Illinois

"Many contemporary realities work against our attempts to establish and cultivate deep, lasting friendships. Add to that our sinful tendencies that lead us to isolate ourselves, and it's no wonder many of us are lonely and, dare I say, friendless. In *Made for Friendship*, Drew Hunter reminds us of the basic human need for true friendships. And through historical, biblical, and practical wisdom, he equips us to pursue and foster the kinds of friendships that will half our sorrows and double our joys. I, for one, am thankful for this much-needed reminder!"

Juan R. Sanchez, Senior Pastor, High Pointe Baptist Church, Austin, Texas; author, *Seven Dangers Facing Your Church*

"Meaningful friendships may be one of the most overlooked areas of church health in our time. If we are going to make disciples, the task will bring with it richness of relationships. This book calls us to relational depth for the sake of our own souls, and for the sake of the gospel."

Matt Boswell, hymnwriter; Pastor, The Trails Church, Celina, Texas

MADE FOR FRIENDSHIP

MADE FOR FRIENDSHIP

THE RELATIONSHIP THAT HALVES OUR
SORROWS AND DOUBLES OUR JOYS

Drew Hunter

Foreword by Ray Ortlund Jr.

:: CROSSWAY®

WHEATON, ILLINOIS

Library of Congress Cataloging-in-Publication Data

Names: Hunter, Drew, author.
Title: Made for friendship : the relationship that halves our sorrows and doubles our joys / Drew Hunter.
Description: Wheaton : Crossway, 2018. | Includes bibliographical references and index. |
Identifiers: LCCN 2017052041 (print) | LCCN 2018016593 (ebook) | ISBN 9781433558207 (pdf) | ISBN 9781433558214 (mobi) | ISBN 9781433558221 (epub) | ISBN 9781433558191 (tp)
Subjects: LCSH: Friendship—Religious aspects—Christianity.
Classification: LCC BV4647.F7 (ebook) | LCC BV4647.F7 H86 2018 (print) | DDC 241/.6762—dc23
LC record available at https://lccn.loc.gov/2017052041

To my friends,
for halving my sorrows and doubling my joys.
And Christina,
my beloved and my best friend (Song 5:16).

CONTENTS

FOREWORD

I love this book! Pastor Drew Hunter is saying things about friendship that I believe in but have never been able to put into words—and powerful words too. For example:

Friendship is the ultimate end of our existence.

Jesus was a man of friendship, because God is a God of friendship.

Each one of us will eventually step into our final week. Some of us will know when we do. If so, we will take a thoughtful glance backward. And we won't wish we put in more hours at work. We won't wish we took more extravagant vacations. We won't wish we spent more time staring at a screen. But we will wish we spent more time with our friends.

What if you could have a friend who knew you better than anyone, better than you even know yourself? And what if, knowing everything, he still loved you, and even liked you? . . . And what if you could have a friend who, by his very relationship with you, would transform you to become a better friend to others? You can. His name is Jesus. He's called the friend of sinners.

Early in my own life, it was my dear dad who showed me the glory of true friendship. I grew up watching my dad love his friends with all his heart, for Jesus's sake. Dad loved to quote Shakespeare, who said,

> Those friends thou hast, and their adoption tried,
> Grapple them to thy soul with hoops of steel.

Now that's how to love a friend—wholeheartedly and permanently! Who wants moderate friendships? Who wants disposable friendships? We all long to be less lonely and more intimate with true friends we can count on. I cannot think of a more urgent need among us today—that we would be friends together through thick and thin, to the glory of God. It's a big part of how people will know we really do belong to Jesus, the friend of sinners (John 13:34–35).

I believe you will find in Pastor Drew Hunter a kindred soul who understands the ups and downs of friendship that you have experienced. He has done his research carefully and thoroughly. He has written sensitively and honestly. He has pulled in writers and voices from many centuries, right up to our present day. Above all, he is biblical and pastoral, showing you God's way into deeper friendships that can last. I joyfully commend to you *Made for Friendship: The Relationship That Halves Our Sorrows and Doubles Our Joys.*

Let's stop living on a starvation diet of friendship! Let the feast begin!

Ray Ortlund Jr.
2017
Immanuel Church
Nashville, Tennessee

INTRODUCTION

One of my worst memories is standing in the high school cafeteria, holding my tray and looking out at several dozen tables encircled with smiling faces, and feeling lonely because I was new and had no friends. One of my happiest memories is sitting by a fire and relaxing with contented joy because I was with my closest friends. Most of us have similar kinds of memories, but we pass them by without any reflection.

You may think that friendship is great—Who isn't for friendship? But you wonder: Do we really need a book about it? Don't we know enough through experience? Or perhaps you think that only lonely people need a book about this.

We don't think much about this topic because we don't think we need to. And as a result, friendship is one of the most familiar yet forgotten relationships in our day.

Most people have friends. But few of us know *true* friendship. Many of us don't know we're missing two of the greatest joys in life: walking with others in true friendship and knowing Jesus as the great Friend.

J. C. Ryle captured the significance of friendship well: "This world is full of sorrow because it is full of sin. It is a dark place. It is a lonely place. It is a disappointing place. The brightest sunbeam in it is a friend. Friendship halves our troubles and doubles our joys."[1] If this is true, there is more to this kind of relationship than many of us know. Most of us think we know true friendship, but few of us do.

This book is about recovering the lost joys of real friendship, and doing so out of the endless resources of knowing our truest Friend. This is not merely a book of handy tips for happier relationships, though you'll find practical wisdom for friendship here. This is also not a collection of quaint quotes for kitchen calligraphy, though we'll certainly uncover gems from church history. Instead, this is about raising our esteem for real friendship so highly that we cannot help but pursue it with enthusiasm and joy.

We'll see that true friendship is worth recovering because no one can enjoy life—true life, life to the full—without it.

If we're going to grab ahold of the meaning of true friendship, we have to answer the most important questions about it: Why do we need it? What is it? What is its ultimate significance? Part 1 (chapters 1 and 2) makes the case that few relationships today are more neglected and few are more needed than true friendship. Part 2 (chapters 3 through 5) uncovers the unique gift of this relationship: chapter 3, the heart of this book, shows the unique joys of friendship—the relationship that C. S. Lewis called "the greatest of worldly goods" and "the chief happiness of life." Then chapter 4 shows what real friendship really looks like. And chapter 5, the most practical of the book, gives the wisdom we need to cultivate it well.

The final part (chapters 6 and 7) uncovers friendship's deepest meaning. First, chapter 6 traces the theme of friendship through the Bible, showing that friendship—friendship with one another and also with God—is at the center of Scripture, the heart of history, and is the ultimate meaning of the universe.

Then chapter 7 leads us to Jesus, the great friend of sinners, the one who lets us all the way in and loves us to the very end. In a statement dense with more significance than many of us may know, he said, "No longer do I call you servants . . . I have called you friends" (John 15:15). Jesus is our Savior and he is our King. He is also our truest Friend. And when we press into this, here's what we find: the greatest power for becoming a better friend is being befriended by the best Friend.

I wrote this book in the hope that it would not only enrich your life as you become captured by this vision of true friendship, but that you would experience this book with others—that the very process of reading this together would strengthen your relationships. In light of this, each chapter concludes with several questions to discuss with a friend or a group.

Finally, although I wrote this with Christians primarily in view, I hope this book will serve as an entryway for some of you to experience the joy of knowing Jesus. I also think you'll be surprised at how relevant the biblical perspective on friendship is to your own life and relationships.

You and I were made for friendship and for fullness of joy. These two purposes belong together. And God gave us the first in order to experience the second, because friendship is a primary way that we tap into the true joy we're all searching for. Friendship is not something we made up; it's something we were made *for*. It's a gift from above. So, let's enjoy it together.

PART I

THE NECESSITY
OF FRIENDSHIP

I

FORGOTTEN FRIENDSHIP

To the Ancients, Friendship seemed the happiest and
most fully human of all loves; the crown of life and
the school of virtue. The modern world, in comparison, ignores it.

C. S. Lewis

If we remove friendship from the world, half of our joy goes
right out with it. This is because friendship is the ultimate end of
our existence and our highest source of happiness. Friendship—
with one another and with God—is the supreme pleasure of life,
both now and forever, and no one can fully enjoy life without it.

Am I overstating things here? If you think so, you'll have
to take it up with someone else. I can't claim much originality
for that paragraph. It is essentially derivative. It paraphrases
perspectives shared by diverse thinkers through the centuries,
from ancient philosophers to great theologians and from modern atheists to devoted Christians. All of these agree: friendship

is not only one of the greatest sources of happiness, but as essayist Joseph Epstein put it, "without friendship, make no mistake about it, we are all lost."[1]

But we don't often esteem friendship this highly. Every other week my wife brings home from the library about twenty books to read with our sons. The most common theme among the children's books is friendship. Yet very few adult books share this focus. Why is that? Is it because the rest of us have friendship figured out? Probably not. True, some groups of people value friendship today; even so, high praise doesn't always translate into thick practice.

One of the central purposes of this book is to make that translation happen—to help us value friendship more highly and then enjoy it more fully.

IN PRAISE OF FRIENDSHIP

So that you know my word is good about that first paragraph, let's take a brief tour of some historical highlights of friendship. We'll start with Augustine, the great theologian and early church father from North Africa. He preached in a sermon, "Two things are essential in this world—life, and friendship. Both must be prized highly, and not undervalued."[2] I can't think of anyone who would disagree with the first necessity, yet the second may be a surprise. But he means it.

The eighteenth-century American pastor Jonathan Edwards also thought deeply about the most important realities in life. He wrote that friendship "is the highest happiness of all moral agents."[3] That's quite a claim, especially from someone who was precise with words: friendship is our *highest* happiness.

Esther Edwards Burr, Jonathan Edwards's daughter and the mother of the third US vice president, Aaron Burr, reflects this truth more personally. She wrote to her friend, "Nothing is more refreshing to the soul (except communication with God himself), than the company and society of a friend."[4] She added that it is "a great mercy that we have any friends—What would this world be with out them? . . . [Friendship] is the life of life."[5]

John Newton, slave trader-turned-pastor and author of the hymn "Amazing Grace" wrote, "I think to a feeling mind there is no temporal pleasure equal to the pleasure of friendship."[6] So if we set up life's pleasures at the starting line, Newton says that friendship finishes first every time.

These and many others not only highly valued friendship; they also deeply enjoyed it. Gregory of Nazianzus and Basil the Great were early church fathers and well-known theologians. But they were also best friends. Their friendship endured through distance and even significant relational challenges. Gregory once wrote to Basil, "The greatest benefit which life has brought me is your friendship."[7] He also wrote, "If anyone were to ask me, 'What is the best thing in life?' I would answer, 'Friends.'"[8]

We know the Reformation-launching Martin Luther, but his friends also knew him for his "table talk"—his lively doctrinal discussions around the dinner table. His wife, Katharina, also enjoyed her own close circle of companions.

We might think of John Calvin pondering great thoughts at a lonely desk, but "a close study of Calvin's career reveals that friendships were the joy of his life."[9] Addressing two of his closest friends, he wrote, "I think that there has never been, in ordinary life, a circle of friends so sincerely bound to each other as we have been in our ministry."[10]

Esther Burr enjoyed deep friendships, especially with her friend Sarah Prince. She wrote to her, "It is a great comfort to me when my friends are absent from me that I have [them] somewhere in the world, and you my dear . . . I esteem you one of the best, and in some respects nearer than any sister I have. I have not one sister I can write so freely to as to you, the sister of my heart."[11] True friends are soul siblings.

The Bible praises friendship with as much vigor as any source, ancient or modern. The story of Scripture is carried along by stories of friendships. Naomi had her Ruth, David his Jonathan, and Paul his Timothy. Jesus too had his Peter, James, and especially John. According to the Bible, friendship is an essential ingredient of the good life. The Scottish pastor Hugh Black said of the book of Proverbs, "There is no book, even in classical literature, which so exalts the idea of friendship, and is so anxious to have it truly valued, and carefully kept."[12]

We've seen this praise of friendship span centuries, genders, and ethnicities; it also spans worldviews. Aristotle, like other ancient Greek philosophers, considered friendship indispensible for life. A. C. Grayling, a modern atheist philosopher, claims, "The highest and finest of all human relationships is, arguably, friendship."[13] One doesn't need to acknowledge the friend of sinners to recognize friendship as one of the deepest pleasures of life.

Yet Christians have a deeper warrant for this kind of praise: friendship is the meaning of the universe. We aren't just made for friendship with each other; we are made for friendship with God. Jesus, the great friend of sinners, came to befriend us. He said to his disciples, "No longer do I call you servants. . . . I have called you friends" (John 15:15). These familiar words are more profound than we may realize. On the eve of his death, Jesus wanted his disciples to know that the cross was not only the greatest demonstration of love but also a cosmic act of friendship. He said, "Greater love has no one than this, that someone lay down his life for his friends" (John 15:13). The cross was history's most heroic act of friendship.

History, it turns out, is nothing less than the story of how the triune God welcomes us into eternal friendship with himself. To be a Christian is to know Jesus—and to be known by him—as a dear friend. As the great nineteenth-century pastor Charles Spurgeon preached, "He who would be happy here must have friends; and he who would be happy hereafter, must, above all things, find a friend in the world to come, in the person of God."[14]

RECOVERING FRIENDSHIP

For most of my life, I never would have made statements like these. I've enjoyed many friendships but not always with great intention. I experienced friendship but never stopped to think directly about it.

This changed when I encountered a few statements about friendship, first in the ancient book of Proverbs, and then from Jesus. Proverbs struck me with its insights and direct statements about it.[15] I eventually came to see the truth in Hugh Black's assessment: "The Book of Proverbs might almost be called a treatise on friendship."[16] I soon realized this was the first time I had devoted even a few minutes to thinking directly about friendship as a topic. Perhaps, like me, you have never spent a full two minutes thinking explicitly about it either. Friendship is, for many of us, one of the most important but least thought about aspects of life.

I also considered Jesus's statements to his disciples about friendship in John 15:12–17. He taught that friendship is the greatest expression of love. It is the meaning of the cross. It is one way in which he wants us to view our relationship with him. It is how he wants us to relate to one another. According to Jesus, the topic of friendship should take us to the heart of the meaning of the cross, history, and love.

This topic is a deep well, and once I started lowering my bucket, it never touched bottom.

Then I wondered: *Why can't I remember hearing anyone talk this way about friendship?* So I turned to church history. It turns out that many have praised and prized friendship above nearly every other earthly good. We've just forgotten our heritage.

A few things have resulted from discovering the biblical and historical riches of friendship. First, the ancients convinced me that they got it right. Aelred of Rievaulx, a twelfth-century author on friendship, wrote, "Absolutely no life can be pleasing without friends."[17] That's a strong claim. *But is it true?* I wondered. So I looked back and reimagined my life without close friends. What came to mind was a life void of all my happiest memories. If I removed friendship from my past, half of my joy would disappear right with it. Now I simply cannot fathom leading a fulfilling life without friends.

If you ask me what's best in life, I'm going to give you names.

Second, these elevated thoughts about friendship carried me to a depressing conclusion: I'm not as good of a friend as I thought. I've since found that this is a typical first response to thinking more deeply about the nature of true friendship. After sharing some observations about this topic with my friend Joe, I asked him for his thoughts. He responded, "I'm a really bad friend." I disagreed, but I also understood—thinking about friendship exposes our own shortcomings. Once we move beyond clichés to consider *true* friendship, we sense we may not be great friends after all. But there's good news: this is only *ini-*

tially disheartening, because discontent pushes us to take steps forward. Awareness is progress.

Finally, I began to approach my relationships much more deliberately. In some seasons of life before this, I didn't think I had the time to cultivate friendship. It was never entirely absent, but I didn't make it central. But we always make time for what we value. So when this new conviction strengthened, it started messing with my schedule. I found myself thinking about my friends, wishing I had more time with them, and connecting with them to make that happen.

That's what I hope happens to you as you read this book: you become a better friend simply as a result of treasuring friendship more highly.

JUST FRIENDS?

What happened to friendship that we must now make such efforts to recover it? For one thing, we've hollowed out and trivialized *friend* and *friendship*. These words now rest lightly on our imaginations. When we honor our closest relationships, we're quicker to grab familial language like *brother* and *sister* than *friend*. I heard someone say to a tight-knit group of Christians, "We're not just friends; we're family." That's true, and the Bible does reference family more than friends; but why the *just*? Friendship didn't seem strong enough to uphold the weight of the moment.

Friendship often feels light, frothy, and sentimental. Friendship quotes sound cliché: "Old friends warm the heart;" "With a little help from my friends;" "Friends are flowers in the garden of life." Charming (perhaps), but not compelling.

We've also connected it to other trivial words: *Chum, pal, buddy. Band of brothers* carries much more gravitas than *band of besties.*

Here's a test: What comes into your mind when you think about friendship with Jesus? His kingly authority calls us to attention, but friendship with Jesus carries little weight. If his kingship connotes strength like a mountain, his friendship reminds us of a light mist. For many, it sounds no different than calling Jesus a little buddy. Some may wonder if the Bible even allows us to call our relationship with God a friendship. It may sound irreverent to you. I'm eager to consider this significant— and significantly misunderstood—topic in the final chapter, but here we can at least note this: The thought of friendship with God rings hollow today because we've already hollowed out the idea of friendship in general. How highly (or lowly) we esteem friendship with God will correlate with how highly (or lowly) we esteem friendship in general—and that is currently at a low point.

We've also stretched out the word *friend*, making it a broad but shallow term. Like a rubber band stretched too far, too long, *friend* is no longer strong enough to hold our closest companions. Friendship should be more like a submarine, holding few and going deep. But we've made it more like a cruise ship, filled with lots of nice people whom we don't know well at all.

We think of friendship more like the word *drink* (a word covering a whole range of liquids) and less like *coffee* (which is specific, and with its own features). We overextend *friend* to the point of ambiguity, applying it to almost everyone we know. Our large number of Facebook friends may be delightful people. But we don't really know. We *do* know all of them are more like contacts and acquaintances than true friends. *Friendship* now refers to so much that it no longer means much.

Friend has become our title for nice people: if she is kind to me, and if she is not my sworn enemy, then she is my friend. We mean well, of course—we want to honor people with the title, and we want to be friendly to everyone. But if *friend* means everyone, then *friend* means nothing.

FRIENDS TO MANY AND FRIENDS TO NONE

It may be that we have made the word *friendship* broad and shallow, but perhaps most of us still have close friendships. The stats aren't reassuring on this one, though: we live increasingly isolated lives.

One study shows that in 1985 the average American had about three friends, defined as people whom we can confide in, people with whom we share the most important things in life. But by 2004, just nineteen years later, the average American only had two close friends, and one in four had no one this close at all.[18] In other words, we experience fewer and fewer deep relationships, and one in four of us have no one (*no one!*) to confide in. Some of us may not wish to open up often, but that's not what this study refers to—this refers to a quarter of us who couldn't do so even if we wanted to. The average American has fewer and fewer real friends. We are increasingly lonely, and very often this lasts for long stretches of life.[19]

And this isn't just an American problem. The UK has now appointed a minister for loneliness to address the growing problem of social isolation.[20] "Rent a friend" companies, first popular in Japan, are now booming in other countries as well. Many people across the globe now pay for a companion to keep them company. Why? Because, as whole societies, we've failed to forge deep relationships.

For some of us, this life looks and feels quite lonely. One past coworker described her daily schedule to me this way: "I work, I go home, and then I watch TV until I fall asleep."

Same lonely rhythm every day. And as we drive through our quiet neighborhoods in the evenings, windows flicker with the familiar blue glow. Many of us know what it's like to sit on our lonely couch, scrolling through endless social media posts. We're connected to many yet connecting with no one. As we see pictures of friends with friends, we wonder if we even have any real friends. "It's a lonely business, wandering the labyrinths of our friends' and pseudo-friends' projected identities, trying to figure out what part of ourselves we ought to project, who will listen, and what they will hear."[21]

On the other hand, many of us don't consider ourselves friendless. We don't *think* we feel particularly lonely. Even now, you may name a handful of people you would call your friends. But how deep are those relationships? How often do you spend time together and talk meaningfully with each other?

One man named Greg told me about a turning point in his life. His wife threw him a surprise party for his fiftieth birthday. Many people came to celebrate since he was well known and well liked. In the days that followed, as he thought back on all the people who came, a sobering insight settled on him: He realized the only person who *really* knew him was his wife. The men who knew him best didn't really know him at all. They didn't know his deepest thoughts, hopes, or uncertainties; they didn't really know *him*—not deeply. And he didn't really know them either. After this, Greg took deliberate steps to go deeper. He started meeting regularly with a group of men from his church, and now he's enjoying truer friendship.

Like Greg's experience, many of us live as a friend to many and yet a friend to no one.

Most of what we call friendship is little more than acquaintanceship. But acquaintanceship is to friendship what snorkeling is to deep-sea diving. Snorkeling is fine, but skimming along the surface isn't exploring the deep. We often float on the surface of our conversations, sharing little more than the most general details of our lives. We note our plans for the day, share a few interesting (or uninteresting) details about our week, offer a few sports or political opinions. But we don't share the climate of our souls. We don't share our struggles with sin. We don't share our experiences of spiritual renewal or admit that we're sitting in a season of darkness. No one knows when our soul feels spiritually chilly. Nor are most of us adept at drawing out others in these ways.

When this becomes the norm, the pattern becomes increasingly difficult to break. To share something disappointing or personally shameful would jar the conversation. And so we acquire the art of acquaintanceship but fail to forge real friendship. We settle for snorkeling and leave the depths unexplored.

Even among those we consider close friends, it's often surprising to consider just how little time we actually spend with them. We sense that our relationships are strong, but we base that sense on time logged in the distant past. Perhaps we went deep years ago, but we've really only snorkeled from time to time since then. Sadly, many of our friends can be considered "longtime friends" because it's been quite a long time since we've experienced true friendship together. Many people have shared with me that although they thought they had friends, they realized they hadn't experienced true friendship in years. One of the saddest sentences I've heard people say is, "I don't really have any friends."

A CORD OF THREE STRANDS . . .

What happened? What makes deep relationships so uncommon and challenging today? Why do we so rarely walk out the front door, enter another human being's home, and enjoy a real, personal, in-the-flesh conversation?

Of course, our own sin affects everything. Sin is antisocial. It curves us inward and it drives us to isolation. The West's hyperindividualistic cultures exacerbate this. Some of us also face unique challenges where we live: cities have their own challenges with transience, smaller communities with set ways, suburbs with isolation. Yet across all locations, three aspects of modern culture create unique barriers to deep relationships: busyness, technology, and mobility.

As we are reminded in Ecclesiastes 4:12, three strands can weave together to form a very strong cord. This triple cord is a powerful image for the value of relationships. Using this metaphor in a different way, these unique modern barriers can weave together in a very isolating way for us. They encircle us like a rope barrier and keep true friendship out of reach. We may overpower one or two of these strands, but as the saying goes, a cord of three strands is not quickly broken.

How about Next Month?

The first strand is busyness. It crowds out friendship from our lives. When I asked a fellow church member if he had any close relationships, he said, "I'm too busy for friends." Between work and family, he didn't think he had any space left. We can commend him for those good commitments, but isn't this like saying we're too busy for water because we're committed to air and food?

Each life stage carries its unique challenges: teenagers with school and sports, young professionals with demanding work hours, parents with competing responsibilities. Where can we find time for friendship if we don't have time for sleep?

Of course, sometimes we're occupied with less redeeming priorities: evening shows, repetitive news cycles, social media, and other potential time wasters. Sometimes we're more lazy-busy than crazy-busy. Either way, we feel strapped. We're time-broke with nothing left for deep relationships.

Even the perception of busyness hinders us from forming strong relationships. One friend said that he never asked me to get together because he assumed I was too busy. When I gave off a perception of busyness, I communicated that I didn't have time for him. Every time you or I tell a would-be deep friend that life is busy, we're really saying that we're too full for friendship.

Nothing says "no chance we'll be friends" like "Let's get together! How about next month?"

Deep Communion vs. Digital Communication

Technology is the second strand. Modern technology is a great tool for keeping up certain aspects of our relationships. Writing emails, sending texts, scanning posts—all of these helpfully *complement* true companionship. But they cannot fully replace it. These are the shallow ends of relationships. We find these tools convenient, but then we're tempted to neglect the deeper waters of shared experiences and face-to-face conversation. Very often the way we use technology leads away from, rather than in to, stronger friendships. We often trade deep communion for digital communication.

Technology can hinder friendship in four ways. First, it often *depersonalizes* communication. We use it to connect, but over time, we feel less, not more, connected. We use it to move closer, but we end up farther away. We trade conversations and experiences for details and updates. We're more connected to more people more often than ever before, but many of our relationships become more superficial and less satisfying.

Second, technology can *disengage* us from real communion. Sometimes when we connect with people through technology, we disconnect from those who are sitting right around us. Friends sit across the table at a coffee shop and enjoy friendship, but not with each other—with the friends on the other end of their phones. Once when I visited a workplace, I stepped into a break room and saw six coworkers sitting around a lunch table. The room was silent. Five of them stared at their phones while the sixth looked at her food. She sat at the table with them, but she ate her lunch alone. Surrounded by peers, she had no one to talk to.

Third, technology *disembodies* conversation. When we engage in person, we experience our friends in unrepeatable and holistic ways. We notice her expressions, intuit her moods, and learn her quirks. Embodied friendship is full of dynamic, real-time, give-and-take interaction. In contrast, digital communication doesn't demand much more than fingers to flit around a keyboard. This has a place of course, but it doesn't match experiencing a person's real presence. For me to see Dane's head roll back and hear his laugh, to talk through personal challenges across the table with Taylor, to see the romance in Christina's eyes, to sense the sincerity in Bill's encouragement, or to pick up the witty humor in Trent's tone—there is simply no digital equivalent.

Finally, technology creates *dependence* on less personal ways of addressing personal issues. Confessing sin and admitting failure, or on the other hand, addressing sin and confronting failure—each of these is challenging, and digital communication seems easier. We take time to craft a statement, and we don't need to worry about immediate reactions. But then we soon prefer to replace a personal meeting with a phone call; a phone call with a voicemail; a voicemail with an email; and an email with a text. Each step smooths the path for the next. Soon we can hardly muster the courage to say anything difficult in person. And without the reassuring eye contact, gentle tone, and responsive clarifications, we often end up adding complications rather than clearing things up.

Friendship in the Rearview Mirror

Increased mobility weaves in as the third strand of this cord. Friendship often requires lots of time together. But we now find it easier than ever to move from one place to another. Education takes us to another town, work transfers families to another state, and retirement draws seniors to sunnier skies.

I moved when I was eleven years old, again when I was fourteen, and four more times since then. Looking back, I would never trade the relationships I formed as a result of those relocations. Still, as moving trucks pulled away, some of my friendships faded in those rearview mirrors. Even the friendships that stuck were altered and more difficult to maintain. I sometimes look back with the "if only" wistfulness about what could have been with some of those friends.

Friendships take time because roots don't go down quickly. And repeated moves can create a "why bother?" mind-set: Why bother to form new friendships here when I already have friendships there? Why sink my roots in when they may soon get pulled up again? Keeping our roots on the surface makes it easier to transplant with the next move. But without deep roots, our relationships cannot grow strong.

So, as busyness, technology, and mobility have increased, friendship has faltered.

FRIENDSHIP IN THE SHADOWS

Churches can serve relational feasts in the midst of this friendship famine. For many, becoming a Christian brings us into a network of new relationships. Churches are often friendly places. But friendliness is not the same as friendship.

Many sit each Sunday on the same sad pew, alone and unknown in a crowd of nice strangers. Many treat Sunday church services more like a drive-through than a restaurant, and still less like a family gathering. Some look for connection through programs and service projects, but nothing can replace the richness of everyday friendship.

Churches often talk about community, which is good. But they don't often talk about friendship, which is not good. We encourage community in general, but we forget friendship in particular. But while we can be "in community" with hundreds, we can only experience true friendship with a few. In truth, a church with deep community is most likely a place in which each person goes deep with a handful of others. These are not isolated cliques (us four and no more) but overlapping networks of relationships.

But why is it that many churches fail to encourage these close relationships? To answer this question, we need to examine an assumption that keeps friendship in the background. Many modern Christians inherited a way of thinking that buries it underneath Christian love. I used to think we should sharply distinguish Christian love and friendship. I heard there were two kinds of love, represented by the Greek words *agape* and *philia*. *Agape* love, I heard, is the highest love. *Philia* love—the love of friendship—is far inferior. *Agape* is unconditional and inclusive, limited to none and extended to all. *Philia* is preferential, limited, exclusive, reserved for only a few.

This contrast leads some to see friendship not merely below *agape* love but even at odds with it. Philosopher Alexander Nehamas wrote, "Friendship and Christian love seem profoundly incompatible with each other."[22] Joseph Epstein quotes Jesus's words from John 15:12—"This is my commandment, that you love one another as I have loved you"—noting that this "may be, at least obliquely, anti-friendship."[23] Why? Because friendship is exclusive, particular, and preferential, while the call to Christian love is all-inclusive. Aren't Christians called to love everyone, not just a few?

Whether or not you've heard it put quite like that, this assumption often keeps friendship in the shadows of Christian love.

The essential question is this: Is friendship really a lesser love? It turns out that it's not. The distinction between Christian love and friendship is far too sharp. For one thing, the Bible often uses *agape* and *philia* interchangeably. Both can refer to the love of God or the love of friends.[24] Most importantly, when Jesus explains the great love command—the very command that some used to promote *agape* love over *friendship* love—he does so in terms of friendship. As we just read, Jesus's famous love command is, "This is my commandment, that you love one another as I have loved you" (John 15:12). But his next words explain this very command in terms of nothing other than friendship: "Greater love [*agape*] has no one than this, that someone lay down his life for his *friends*" (v. 13)! According to Jesus, no love exceeds friendship love. He says, essentially, "Love one another as friends, just as I've loved you as friends."

Friendship love is, therefore, an essential part of Christian love. Far from being at odds with Christian love, friendship is a central way in which we live it out. Christian love and true friendship belong together; they are not enemies but friends. We should feel no ultimate tension between the two: Christian love expresses friendliness to all and enjoys friendship with a few.

WHEN EVERYONE MISSES THEIR FRIENDS

Bronnie Ware served as an Australian nurse for several years. As she assisted patients in their final weeks of life, she recorded their dying epiphanies and eventually wrote her observations in the book, *The Top Five Regrets of the Dying*. Ware noticed people's phenomenal clarity of vision at the end of their lives.

She asked her patients—people just like you and me, except that they knew they only had a few weeks left—if they would do anything differently if they could go back. She heard several recurring answers.

One of the greatest regrets of the dying? "I wish I had stayed in touch with my friends." She explains:

> Often they would not truly [realize] the full benefits of old friends until their dying weeks and it was not always possible to track them down. Many had become so caught up in their own lives that they had let golden friendships slip by over the years. There were many deep regrets about not giving friendships the time and effort that they deserved. [25]

In our final weeks, a lot of what we now care so much about will quickly evaporate. But relationships will remain an immovable priority. Because, in the end, "everyone misses their friends when they are dying."[26]

In his final days, the apostle Paul wrote to his longtime friend Timothy. We have, as far as we know, his final letter. And with his last words, he wrote, "Do your best to come to me soon" (2 Tim. 4:9). And, again: "Do your best to come before winter" (v. 21).

Each one of us will eventually step into our final week. Some of us will know when we do. If so, we will take a thoughtful glance backward. And we won't wish we had put in more hours at work. We won't wish we had taken more extravagant vacations. We won't wish we had spent more time staring at a screen. But we will wish we had spent more time with our friends.

Because, as we'll see next, friends are among life's matchless necessities.

QUESTIONS FOR REFLECTION AND DISCUSSION

1. Which quotation from the first section stood out to you the most? Why?

2. Why is it particularly challenging for us to go deeper than superficialities in conversation?

3. Which of the problematic "three strands" (busyness, technology, mobility) is the biggest obstruction to friendship for you? Why? Can you think of other obstructions?

4. If this were your final week, which three friends would you miss most? What is one concrete step you can take this week to strengthen each friendship?

2

THE EDENIC ACHE

Two things are essential in this world—life, and friendship. Both must be prized highly, and not undervalued. They are nature's gifts. We were created by God that we might live; but if we are not to live solitarily, we must have friendship.

Augustine

Human life requires few necessities: water, food, and oxygen. Other things like coffee, furniture, and even the Internet are nice, but ultimately optional. But what about friendship? We often think of it as a social luxury—important, surely—but *necessary*? But what if friendship is more like oil to a car's engine than leather on its seats? What if life without friendship only takes us so far down the road until we start breaking down? What if it's not just an optional theme in life but part of what it means to be human? Charles Spurgeon preached,

> Friendship seems as necessary an element of a comfortable existence in this world as fire or water, or even air itself. A man may drag along a miserable existence in proud solitary dignity, but his life is scarce life, it is nothing but an existence.[1]

If you want to call friendship a luxury, that's fine. But then make sure you also call air a luxury. There are few true necessities in life. Friendship is one of them.

PRESCRIPTION: FRIENDSHIP

How do we test this claim? If friendship were necessary, how would we know? For starters, we could consider what happens when we don't have it. When we imagine such a scenario, we find that friendlessness isn't just depressing; it's actually quite dangerous. When we come unglued from others socially, we come unraveled emotionally, psychologically, and even physically. This is because we're embodied beings. Our mind and emotions are mysteriously interconnected with our bodies. So when we experience loneliness, it affects every part of us.

This is true for everyone—men and women, extroverts and introverts. The former US Surgeon General Vivek Murthy said that when he saw patients, the most common illness was not cancer or heart disease but loneliness.[2] Loneliness is a hazard to our health, and increasingly so with age. Loneliness "poses a particular threat to the very old, quickening the rate at which their faculties decline and cutting their lives shorter."[3]

Thankfully, what loneliness removes, friendship restores. My wife's grandmother went through a several-month stretch of loneliness. As she stayed home every day, her health and happiness slowly declined. Then she moved into an assisted-living home. She made fast friends with her neighbors, quickly regained her appetite, and started feeling well again. Here's what this shows us: when loneliness unravels us, relationships put us back together.

Friendship is the missing medicine for many of our afflictions.

The ancient wisdom of Proverbs cautioned against isolation long ago: "Whoever isolates himself seeks his own desire; he breaks out against all sound judgment" (Prov. 18:1). People may have their reasons for seclusion, but they have not followed the path of wisdom. I used to imagine a sage as a lonely graybeard who lived somewhere up on a great mountain. I clearly didn't get that image from the Bible. The wise life looks like a journey with and for others, not by and for oneself.

On the other hand, we may fill our lives with people and yet never experience true friendship. According to Proverbs 18:24, "A man of many companions may come to ruin, but there is a friend who sticks closer than a brother." Proverbs tells us not to measure relational health by how many people we know but by how deeply we go with them.

The wise person journeys through life neither alone nor in an impersonal crowd, but side by side with friends.

The great assumption behind Proverbs' vision of the good life is this: God made the world, and he made it to work a certain way. Therefore, the wise embrace his design. They know how to live well in God's world. They see reality clearly, and they adjust to it. And if Proverbs emphasizes friendship to the point that it "might almost be called a treatise on friendship,"[4] then this topic deserves our closest attention. Friendship is essential for the good life because God wove it into the fabric of the world.

THE ACHE FOR FRIENDSHIP

The Bible's first pages show our inescapable need for relationships. Several times the creation story in Genesis 1 repeats the phrase "and God saw that it was good" (1:4, 10, 12, 18, 21, 25). It climaxes with the seventh occurrence: "It was *very* good" (v. 31). Then in chapter 2, we read of one thing that is *not good*: "It is not good that the man should be alone" (2:18). Adam, the first human, lives, but he lives in isolation. And that's a problem. As Martin Luther put it, "God created man for society and not for solitude."[5] Thus we can each make this statement our own: it is not good that [*your name*] should be alone.

God announces Adam's problem and then parades the animals before him. Why this, and why now? So that Adam might feel his need for community. The animal parade made a point: apparently pets alone won't do. Even "man's best friend" passed by without special notice. This was because Adam didn't need a pet; he needed another person. Animals are special, but human friendship is of a higher order.

This takes place *before* sin enters the world. That's significant. Satan has not yet slithered in, the forbidden fruit has no fingerprints, and Adam's conscience remains clear. The first problem in human history, the first problem on the pages of Scripture, the first problem in any human life, was not sin—it was solitude.

This means that the not-goodness of Adam's aloneness was not a result of his fallenness. Adam stood there in Eden without fault, yet he also stood alone and therefore incomplete. He was missing something essential enough to warrant the divine declaration of "not good." Adam, untouched by sin, needed a friend. Tim Keller notes,

> Adam was not lonely because he was imperfect, but because he was perfect. The ache for friends is the one ache that is not the result of sin. . . . This is one ache that is part of his perfection. . . . God made us in such a way that we cannot enjoy paradise without friends. God made us in such a way

that we cannot enjoy our joy without human friends. Adam had a perfect quiet time every day, 24 hours. He never had a dry one, and yet he needed [friends].[6]

Every soul reverberates with the echoes of this Edenic ache for friendship. It's an ancient and primal longing. We are inescapably communal.

The opening chapters of Genesis cast a vision of the good life, full of *shalom*—a Hebrew concept referring in its fullest sense to flourishing, joy, and harmony. And this *shalom* exists between God, humanity, and creation. Each sphere of the physical world—land, sea, and sky—teems with life. Yet Adam stands in the middle of this exuberant wonder world—alone. Adam has life, and that's a start. But he also needs community.

Since Adam doesn't linger in isolation for long, we can't be sure how this "not good" state would play out over time. But we do know what happens when this trajectory is followed, when we force someone away from human contact for months. It's not good. Prison officials call solitary confinement, "the prison within the prison."[7] A central feature of solitary confinement is social isolation. It results in increased anxiety, depression, and mental illness. Isolation isn't negative attention; it's *no* attention, which is often worse. Solitary confinement unravels our humanity.

These dynamics compelled the main character in the movie *Castaway* to forge a friendship with Wilson—a volleyball. True, befriending a ball already betrays a bit of insanity, but this little companion brought some normalcy to Chuck Noland's increasingly crazy mind. How do you answer the "what five things would you take to a desert island" question? If we want to keep our minds, at least one answer must be someone's name. God made us in such a way that solitude and sanity cannot coexist for long. We will eventually only keep one or the other.

Of course complete isolation, whether in a prison or on an island, is not likely your future or mine. But our experiences of loneliness lean in that direction. Its trajectory is misery. Its end is dehumanization.

THE DIVINE AFFIRMATION OF FRIENDSHIP

So, on the sixth day God made Adam and he made Eve—the first friendship—and behold, it was very good.

It was Eve's presence that finally made the creation "*very* good." Consider when she arrives in the story. The creation account has two parts: *part one* overviews the entire seven-day creation week (Gen. 1:3–2:4). On the sixth day of that week, God made humanity—both Adam *and* Eve. Only after the completion of the sixth day, with Adam and Eve both created, do we hear the climactic "very good" (1:31).

After this, *part two* of the creation account rewinds back into the midst of that sixth day and zooms into God's creation of Adam and then Eve. There, in the middle of the sixth day, God creates Adam first and then, before he creates Eve, he announces, "It is not good that the man should be alone" (2:18).

In other words, the order of events is: (1) God creates Adam, (2) God announces that it is "not good," (3) God creates Eve, and (4) now, with Adam and Eve together, everything is "very good." Here's the point: as the creation week moves along, the whole creation is not pronounced "very good" until God addresses the one thing that is not good—Adam's isolation. This shows us that a world without friendship is not complete; it's not yet *very* good.

You may be asking one or two questions at this point.

First, isn't *marriage* God's answer to Adam's aloneness problem? In other words, aren't marriages (in particular) and not human relationships (in general) God's provision for Adam's solitude? We do learn that Eve's role as a spouse is an essential provision for Adam. After God created Adam and Eve, he commissioned them to "be fruitful and multiply and fill the earth and subdue it" (1:28). Adam could not fulfill this task on his own, and God provided marriage in order to fulfill this mission of multiplication.

However, when God said, "It is not good that the man should be alone," he didn't just highlight Adam's need for a wife but also the general problem of man's *aloneness*. Eve's presence solved this problem in two ways: First, she met Adam's need for companionship. Yes, as a wife, but also as a friend. Marriages are ideally the deepest of friendships. The bride in Song of Solomon declares, "This is my beloved and this is my friend" (Song 5:16). Second, Eve solved the problem of humanity's isolation by multiplying society with Adam. Eve became the bridge between one isolated man and a populated globe. Through Eve, humanity would fill the earth with community. So, Eve met Adam's need for companionship, and she also provided the means of creating a world of friendship.

The other question you may be asking is this: Why did Adam need someone else when he already had God? The first question was essentially: Isn't *marriage* enough? And now the second is like it: Isn't *God* enough? Does this not turn friendship into idolatry, as though we need something else besides God to be satisfied or complete?

This is an important question. From one perspective, God *is* enough. Take everything away but Christ, and we still have everything.

> Whom have I in heaven but you?
>   And there is nothing on earth I desire besides you. . . .
> God is the strength of my heart and my portion forever.
>   (Ps. 73:25–26)

"Foes may hate and friends disown me, Show Thy face and all is bright."[8] And yet there stood Adam, with the great Friend and every noble pleasure, and it was not good.

Why? Because God made us to fully enjoy him *as* creatures.[9] In other words, we experience God in a way that fits with how he made us. He made us as humans, and we experience pleasure in human, creaturely ways. We enjoy God, then, in the way that *humans* enjoy God. And one way in which we enjoy him *as humans* is through his gifts—and chief among them is friendship. We honor God when we receive this with gratitude.

We thank God *for* friendship, we treasure God *above* friendship, and we enjoy God *through* friendship.

TRUE SPIRITUALITY

Our very creaturely pleasures are, in fact, *spiritually* significant. For much of my life I didn't connect friendship with spirituality. Spirituality was for worship services, Bible reading, and prayer. Friendship, with its conversations and laughter and fun, didn't seem particularly spiritual. But this was misguided. We can't divorce the spiritual from the creational. Instead, we should measure spiritual maturity by seeing how we become more, not less, enchanted with God's glory in his gifts.

In other words, when Paul requested (twice) that his close friend visit him at the end of his life, that wasn't spiritually weak of him. No, his request rose out of his deep maturity. Paul was utterly content with Christ as his great Friend. Yet he also asked for another friend. John Stott commented,

> One sometimes meets super-spiritual people who claim that they never feel lonely and have no need of human friends, for the companionship of Christ satisfies all their needs. But human friendship is the loving provision of God for

> mankind. . . . Wonderful as are both the presence of the
> Lord Jesus every day and the prospect of his coming on the
> last day, they are not intended to be a substitute for human
> friendships. . . . When our spirit is lonely, we need friends.
> . . . To admit this is not unspiritual; it is human.[10]

Is this not a central point on the Bible's very first page? Creation's abundance teaches that God takes pleasure in pleasing us. "Everything created by God"—things like raspberries and sunsets and music and *friendship*—"is good, and nothing is to be rejected if it is received with thanksgiving" (1 Tim. 4:4). When we thank God for friendship, we aren't praising *friends*; we're praising God *for* friends.

As God shows his goodness through his generosity, we give him glory through our gratitude.[11]

MADE FOR "WITH-NESS"

It's one thing to affirm that friendship is beneficial, important, and so forth. But Genesis shows us more. It shows us that friendship is indispensible. Why? Because we are made in the image of the God who eternally exists as a triune fellowship of love.

"God said, 'Let us make man in our image, after our likeness'" (Gen. 1:26). This plural surprises us: *our* image. Why not *my* image? This implies that God is communal.[12] Looking back from the vantage point of the New Testament, we see that God is triune: the one God eternally exists as three persons—Father, Son, and Holy Spirit. This God is utterly unique as the Creator of all things, yet he also made humanity in his image. We are made in the image of the God who exists in communal love. This is the deepest reason for friendship. Our nature as God's image bearers, as those he created to represent him and rule over creation, entails friendship. Because of this, God embedded friendship in our DNA. "We are made for 'withness.'"[13]

This highlights the uniqueness of the true God. If Allah created Adam, then Genesis could just as well have read, "Adam was alone, and Allah saw that it was very good." Why? Because Allah is solitary. A solitary Adam could reflect that image perfectly well. Selfless love could never be one of Allah's essential qualities, for there has not always been another person to love.

But "God is love" because God is triune. There was never a time when love was not, because there was never a time when the Trinity was not. To be made in God's image—the God who *is* love—means that we, at the creaturely level, are wired for relationships. God made us to enjoy him and reflect him, and a beautiful implication is that we were made to enjoy a life of communal love.

Adam cannot, then, reflect God's beauty alone—not because it's difficult without a helper but because it's impossible without an *other*.

"So God created man in his own image . . . male and female he created *them*" (1:27). Another curious plural: not, "Let *me* make man in *my* image . . . so God . . . created *him*," but "Let *us* make man in *our* image . . . so God . . . created *them*" (vv. 26–27). One person alone could not reflect the fullness of God's communal image.

What does this mean for us today? We long for friendship because we're made like God. "The less you want friends," Tim Keller has observed, "the less like God you are."[14] Therefore, one way that we reflect God is by entering and enjoying friendship's pleasures. God's image is less reflected in a hermit's home than it is around a meal with laughter and love.

YOU ARE NOT A ROCK

To shift the posture of your life away from others—whether through purposeful withdrawal or passive isolation—is to turn away from your very design.

This is why friendlessness is dehumanizing. Without relationships of love, we eventually become more like animals. In his classic book on friendship, Aelred of Rievaulx wrote,

> Those who claim that their lives should be such as to console no one and to be a burden or the occasion of grief to no one, who derive no joy from others' success and inflict no bitterness on others with their own [sin], I would call not human beings but beasts. They have only one goal: neither to love nor to be loved by anyone.[15]

Paul Simon compared deliberate isolation to being like a rock. In his song "I Am a Rock," he wrote,

> I have no need of friendship
> Friendship causes pain.[16]

But, then, a rock isn't quite human. Rocks don't feel pain, true, but they also don't know pleasure. C. S. Lewis observed:

> Love anything, and your heart will certainly be wrung and possibly broken. If you want to make sure of keeping it intact, you must give your heart to no one, not even to an animal. Wrap it carefully round with hobbies and little luxuries; avoid all entanglements; lock it up safe in the casket or coffin of your selfishness. But in that casket—safe, dark, motionless, airless—it will change. It will not be broken; it will be unbreakable, impenetrable, irredeemable. . . . The only place outside Heaven where you can be perfectly safe from all the dangers and perturbations of love is Hell.[17]

Hell is the opposite of life, so it contains no trace of love. Life, on the other hand—abundant life—only opens up and shares its deepest pleasures when we're in community. Flourishing requires friendship.

We all know something of unmet longings for close relationships. Some of us have known friendship but lost it, perhaps through betrayal, perhaps through our own mistakes. Maybe we've drifted away from certain friends so slowly that we are only now noticing just how far apart we are.

Each one of us feels the pain of the Edenic ache, some of us more acutely than others. But we should not salt the wound by calling this a sign of weakness. If you desire true friendship, it is not because you are weak; it is because you're not a rock. You are made in the image of the God of exuberant love. You are most like God, and you are most truly human when you want friendship. Your unmet longings for friendship are not evidence of a deficiency; they are signs of your dignity.

God made you for friendship.

FRIENDS . . . WHO NEEDS 'EM?

Everyone, apparently, needs friends. Since relationality is essential to our humanity, there is no gender or personality type or marital status or age group or life stage that can forgo friendship—not without harm. No one with a fully flourishing life treats true community as a mere luxury. Still, friendship will look different for different life stages, personality types, and so forth. And each life situation comes with its own set of strengths and challenges.

If you're an extrovert, for example, you probably make fast friends with many people. However, a vision of true friendship pushes you to go deeper. Without that intentionality, you may gain many companions but have no close friends. I'm more introverted, so I enjoy relational depth more than breadth. I find that I need to make sure I don't neglect other people as I enjoy my smaller circle of closest friends. Introverts also like to be alone in order to recharge, but some batteries, if perpetually plugged into the wall, lose their capacity. The refreshment I receive from being alone partly exists for the sake of reengaging with and encouraging others.

Young people often build their lives around relationships. But over time, as people approach middle age, many find themselves without deep friendships. When older people cross the vocational finish line into retirement, some look around and realize they weren't running alongside anyone else; all their companions split off and took different routes. Of course, this isn't always the case—many seniors at my church have lively networks of everyday relationships. But for too many of us, our best years of friendship remain in the past. When many think of their best years of friendship, they think of their childhood. Friendship is more of a past memory than a present reality.

Marriage also adds new challenges. I remember one man telling me that he didn't think he needed friends once he got married. He thought of his wife as the only companion he needed. Like him, very often one's spouse becomes not just one's *best* friend but also one's *only* friend. But when he began to meet regularly with a group of men, he soon realized that he didn't know what he was missing until he had it.

This is why my wife and I committed to freeing one another up for friendships. This comes at a cost, of course. Because we have younger children, I need to be home when she's out with friends, and she needs to be home when I'm out with friends. We also lose that time together. But our marriage is ultimately better for it because relationships enrich our lives. We return encouraged from time with others and with stories to share. When we strengthen the bonds of our other relationships, we find our bond of marriage strengthened as well. Friends make us happier and whole, and that enriches every part of life.

Single men and women often have more flexibility and time for relationships. Yet if you're single, perhaps you've also felt unable to connect with those who are married. Even when married men and women forge friendships outside of their own marriage, they often gravitate toward other married couples. Additionally, many churches have so highly valued marriage over singleness that the unmarried feel left on the outside of relationships. This should change. Churches have a unique opportunity to affirm the goodness and challenges of singleness, and to promote friendships among those with or without a spouse.

But married and single people will often need to sort through their different expectations. If you're single, you may have more time and flexibility. You may expect your married friend to get together as much as she did when she was single. Friendship across different life stages requires adjusting expectations and extending grace.

Men and women also experience friendship differently. Generally speaking, women major on face-to-face conversations, while men emphasize side-by-side experiences. But full friendships include a rounded mix of both. If you're a side-by-side type, linger after the activity and ask your friends what recently encouraged or discouraged them. If you default to face-to-face interactions, plan some activities to build memories together.

Friendship will look different for each of life's stages, but it remains essential for all.

CONCLUSION

Adam was made for friendship. The second Adam, sharing fully in our humanity, needed friendship no less than the first. Jesus did not live alone. He and his disciples walked dusty roads together, engaged in lengthy conversations, and feasted in homes. Jesus grieved over the death of Lazarus, his friend (John 11:11). In the most distressing moment of Jesus's life before the cross—his anguish in the garden of Gethsemane—he wanted his closest friends near, and he was disappointed when they weren't. This world has never known a person more deeply spiritual than Jesus, and he was a man of deep relationships.

Jesus was a man of friendship, because God is a God of friendship.

The very existence of friendship in the world portrays something profound: at the center of the universe is a love so great that it must be shared. Through friendship—friendship with God and with one another—God shares with us something of his own eternal and effusive joy. Our enjoyment of relationships—even our most ordinary moment with our most ordinary companion—is more profound than we often realize: it is a reflection of God's own infinitely joyous fellowship as Father, Son, and Spirit.

Many of us carry disappointments from our relationships. But we feel this discouragement because God planted this glory deep in our hearts. We long for more because God made us for more.

It's time, then, to consider just what it is that makes friendship one of life's greatest gifts.

QUESTIONS FOR REFLECTION AND DISCUSSION

1. When in your life have you felt most isolated or alone? Did you experience other mental or emotional difficulties at this time?

2. What are two or three aspects of friendship that you are most thankful to God for?

3. Have you experienced disappointments in friendship that led you to become a bit more hard, more closed off, to the vulnerability of friendship? What is the danger to letting this hardness set?

4. Circle the words that describe your personality and life situation:

   single   married
   male   female
   younger   middle-age   older
   introvert   extrovert

Note one particular challenge that each of these brings to your pursuit of friendship. For each of these challenges, note one step you can take to add depth to your friendships.

5. Do you tend to value side-by-side experiences or face-to-face conversations? What is one way you can try to add a bit more balance to your default way of experiencing friendship?

PART 2

THE GIFT OF FRIENDSHIP

3

THE GREATEST OF
WORLDLY GOODS

This world is full of sorrow because it is full of sin.
It is a dark place. It is a lonely place. It is a disappointing place. The brightest sunbeam in it is a
friend. Friendship halves our troubles and doubles
our joys.

J. C. Ryle

The laughter subsided for a moment. I leaned in to stir the em-
bers and shift the pine logs. Then the flames rose again to il-
lumine the faces of thirteen other men sitting around the fire.
We were sharing our favorite memories from our past years of
adventures and camping trips.

A few of us recounted the year of the flies. We had back-
packed three miles to camp along Lake Superior's shoreline.
We reached the site and began setting up our tents. But dozens,

then hundreds, then thousands of flies steadily gathered to us. They were biting flies and they won, so we abandoned our site and hiked three miles out in the midday heat. But the flies stayed with us. A few hundred of them swarmed around and frequently bit us.

We also remembered Brian's walk across a log over the ravine with a thirty-foot drop. We remembered how three of us had lost our wedding rings in rivers. We remembered capsizing canoes, swinging from vines, pushing over dead trees, and leaping over small waterfalls.

The smoke rose as we continued to share and laugh. That night we were camping on the edge of Bowen Lake in the Colorado mountains. Most of us have done this together nearly every year, some of us for about fifteen years. We call it MEWALO—Men's Extended Weekend Adventure Liberation Organization (in celebration of awkward acronyms). Every year we choose a new place for a new adventure. Each trip is one of our high points of the year, and we enjoy it for one primary reason: because we're together. Most of us keep in touch or connect in different ways through the year, and then we all meet for this extended weekend in the summer.

One of my friends, Tim, says that MEWALO is like a sea anchor to the soul. Most of us are aware of only one kind of anchor—a weight that tethers us to the seabed. But another kind, a sea anchor, steadies a boat in stormy weather. It helps a boat slow down and keeps it from drifting and thrashing around in the waves. Because of the way we structure these trips—days in the wilderness, minimal technology, no distractions, life-on-life with soul-on-soul conversations—we inevitably reflect on our lives. We find ourselves steadied, reminded of what we believe is true, good, and beautiful in life, even when it's hard. It's also refreshing. We laugh more across those few days than we might in any other given month.

C. S. Lewis wrote to his lifelong friend, Arthur Greeves: "Friendship is the greatest of worldly goods. Certainly to me it is the chief happiness of life."[1] Those are remarkable statements, but few would make them today. Did Lewis know something about friendship that we don't? Did he experience it in a way that many of us haven't?

If we're going to recover real friendship, we need to know what could make someone praise it like that. How do good friends give us the good life? Here are six unique joys of real friendship.

I. DOUBLING OUR JOYS

First, good friends double our joys. They make life better because they make us happier. We just read that C. S. Lewis called friendship the chief happiness in life. He also claimed, more universally, that friendship causes "perhaps half of all the happiness in the world."[2] Maybe that's hyperbole. But even so, it gestures toward the truth.

Arthur Brooks studied the key contributors to people's happiness in America (the nation that etched "the pursuit of happiness" onto its foundation). Other than our own genes and circumstances, Brooks found four factors that correlate most closely with happiness: faith, family, meaningful work, and friends.[3] A couple of those may not surprise you. But what about friends? I would have expected a six-digit income, a mansion on the beach, international fame, or even the pleasures of hobbies and recreation. But they didn't make the list. Friendship did.

Think back on your life for a few moments. Consider it as a trek across a mountain range with all of its peaks and valleys.

What do you see at those highest and happiest points? When I look at mine, I see the faces of my closest relationships.

As I zoom in to those high points, I also see various activities: romping through the woods with Brett and riding through puddled streets with Derek in childhood; late-night conversations in college with Taylor and Jonny; long walks after graduate school classes with Scott; MEWALO trips each year with Ricky, Jeff, Aaron, and the rest of the group. I'm sure I would still enjoy each of these activities alone or with acquaintances. But without friends, I wouldn't remember any one of them as a high point. My life's most nostalgic moments, the ones I most wish I could relive, always involve close relationships.

A few evenings each year I meet up with my friends Dane, Don, and Joe. Since I don't live near them anymore, sometimes I drive three hours each way in order to spend a few hours with them. But I've never questioned the tradeoff. Bratwursts sizzle on the grill, logs crackle in the fire, and a certain kind of palpable, contented joy calmly settles on us, shaped by our long history and strong affection.

We sometimes refer to our meeting as an experience of inaugurated eschatology. That is, when part of the inexpressible joy of the age to come breaks into today. According to the Bible, the eternal future of God's people will not consist in floating on clouds with harps. Yes, we go to heaven when we die. But when Jesus returns, our bodies will be raised from the dead, and we'll live on a new earth to enjoy physical, communal life to the full. Our friendships today foreshadow the joy of that coming new creation.

The best description I can give to explain these moments comes from C. S. Lewis. He described gathering with close friends as being enfolded in an "Affection" (capital *A*). He wrote,

Those are the golden sessions . . . when our slippers are on,
our feet spread out towards the blaze and our drinks at our
elbows; when the whole world, and something beyond the
world, opens itself to our minds as we talk . . . at the same
time an Affection mellowed by the years enfolds us. Life—
natural life—has no better gift to give.[4]

One of life's greatest pleasures is the inexplicable atmosphere of
joy, or gratefulness, or *shalom*—I'm not sure we have a word for
it in English—that settles over a gathering of longtime friends.

My brother Trent recently moved away from Albuquerque,
New Mexico. He had forged deep and rich relationships there.
After his last few days packing up with friends, he sent me this
note: "Friendship. Tasting heaven in the here and now. Pulling out
of Albuquerque for the last time in a long time, and this captures
it for me." True friendship gives a taste of heaven on earth—even
when you're doing something as mundane as loading a truck.

So far I've focused on how friendship *adds* happiness to our
lives. It slides in right along other joys and makes life better. But
friendship also *multiplies* our happiness, because it consum-
mates our other joys. When we experience something exciting,
we spontaneously share it with others. The four-year-old version
sounds like, "Daddy, watch this!" The twenty- and forty- and
sixty-year-old version sounds more like, "Did you watch the
game last night?" "Did you see the sky this morning?" "Look
at this picture of what I did yesterday." Why do we do this?
Because telling a friend about what brings us joy increases our
joy. It carries that happiness to its completion.

A joy unshared is a joy unfulfilled. And a joy shared is a joy
doubled.

This is why, when our friends die, the pain cuts deep. It hurts
mainly because we lose their presence, but it also hurts because

we can no longer share our joys with them. We finally reach a milestone, and the person who would most appreciate it can't. So our joy rises, but it remains unfulfilled.

Without friendship, our happiest moments hit a ceiling.

I think of Michael Jordan in the first moments after he and the Bulls won their championship game in 1996. The clock ran down, the stadium erupted with cheers, and the team lit up with celebration. But Jordan grabbed the ball and then laid facedown on the court. After a few moments, he slowly stood up, walked off the court into the locker room, and laid on the ground again, clutching the ball and crying. It was Father's Day, and it was the first championship he had won since "Pops," whom he called his best friend, had died. In an interview several minutes later, he explained his emotion: "This is for Daddy." Of all his accomplishments in basketball, Michael Jordan affirmed that this was *the* accomplishment, because it represented his father. It was a wonderful moment, but his happiness hit a ceiling. His joy surged, but it was not full because he couldn't share it with his father, his best friend.

2. HALVING OUR SORROWS

Second, good friends cut our sorrows in half. You may feel like the rainy days in your soul far outnumber the sunnier ones. We all walk through seasons of darkness. And when we do, a close friend is like a sun's ray that pierces through the clouds to give a shaft of warm light. Friends ease our sorrows in two ways: they give us their presence, and they give us their words.

First, friends encourage us with their presence. Martin Luther, no stranger to sadness, often encouraged friends in their own discouragement. He repeatedly exhorted people to flee isolation. He wrote, "Solitude produces melancholy. When we are alone the worst and saddest things come to mind. . . . We interpret everything in the worst light."[5] Maybe you can relate to Chester Bennington, Linkin Park's former lead singer, who said in an interview, "When I'm in my own head, this place right here, this skull between my ears—that is a bad neighborhood. And I should not be in there alone. . . . I don't say nice things to myself. There is another Chester in there that wants to take me down."[6] He said that when he was not with family and friends, when he was not getting outside of himself, he spiraled downward. But he was happier when he was with the people he loved.

As I write this, my wife, Christina, is out with some of her friends. A few hours ago she told me that they invited her out to dinner. She was in a discouraged mood, so she planned to stay home. Against that inclination, we decided this was the reason she *should* go. We've learned that friends, magnet-like, pull us out of ourselves. So when one of us feels like our downcast mood disqualifies us and should keep us away from friends, we remember that friendship is actually what we most need.

When we're left to ourselves, we quickly descend into the dark places of our souls. This is why we need good companions who stay with us and who empathize with us. When they join with us in our downcast moments, they may not feel like they're doing much, but they're holding a candle in our darkness. Their presence says that they know us and that they love us. They help us turn outward, away from our own gloomy thoughts.

Many Christians know William Cowper's hymn "There Is a Fountain Filled with Blood." But most don't know how he endured depression throughout his life. John Newton became his pastor, counselor, and friend. Newton saw his inclinations toward depression, so he invited Cowper to take long walks with him as he visited homes. Newton stayed close to

Cowper when he dropped into deeper despair. Newton once sacrificed his vacation to make sure he didn't leave him alone. He also invited Cowper to live with him for over a year until he steadied.

We never get the sense that Cowper felt like a project. Newton wrote,

> The Lord who had brought us together had so knit our hearts and affections that for nearly twelve years . . . we were seldom separated for twelve hours at a time when we were awake and at home. The first six I passed in daily admiring and trying to imitate him; during the second six I walked pensively with him in the valley of the shadow of death.[7]

When Newton moved to London for another pastoral role, they often wrote to one another. Cowper called Newton "the friend of my heart" and wrote, "There is no day in which you are excluded from my thoughts."[8] Neither of them viewed their relationship primarily through the lens of pastor and parishioner. They were friends. And friends encourage one another through their faithful presence.

Second, friends ease our sorrows through encouraging words. The book of Proverbs says, "A man's spirit will endure sickness, but a crushed spirit who can bear?" (Prov. 18:14). In other words, if you know the oppressive, downward pull of depression, you'd trade it for the flu, and you'd do it with a smile.

What can we offer to a depressed friend? "Anxiety in a man's heart weighs him down," Proverbs observes, "but a good word makes him glad" (12:25). A central purpose of friendship is the ministry of encouragement, the service of giving these "good words" that make the soul glad. We come to one another bearing words of hopeful truth, words of comfort, words that bring joy. Our speech can change the climate of our friend's soul.

God's encouragement comes to us through the words of Scripture, and those words often come to us through friends. When we're discouraged, we need an outside word. And we need to hear it in the familiar voice of a friend.

I remember when my friend Ryan called me when he was discouraged. He said the reason he called was for me to remind him of the gospel. He knew it well, but he also knew he needed it to come to him from the outside. He needed to hear again what he already knew. So I shared what had encouraged me that morning from the Bible. I read God's gracious words for his rebellious people: "You are precious in my eyes, and honored, and I love you" (Isa. 43:4). We considered God's love in Christ's cross and resurrection, and then we prayed. We both ended the conversation feeling renewed.

So friends lift us in our sadness in these two ways: by being with us and by encouraging us with hope. John Bunyan illustrated how these work together in his book *Pilgrim's Progress*. Christian faces many trials as he journeys toward the Celestial City. Along the way, he and his friend Hopeful are captured by Giant Despair, who locks them in his dungeon. When Christian sinks into despair, Hopeful gently exhorts him, gives him hope, and prays with him. Because of this, Christian's heart strengthens with confidence. He remembers the Key of Promise in his coat. It unlocks every door. With Hopeful's encouragement, Christian turns the locks and both friends burst into freedom.[9]

When we feel locked in a dungeon of depression, the keys of God's promises lead us out. In all our sorrows we remember, "For those who love God all things work together for good"

(Rom. 8:28). We "do not lose heart" because "though our outer self is wasting away, our inner self is being renewed day by day" (2 Cor. 4:16). We remember, as Cowper wrote, "Behind a frowning providence, [God] hides a smiling face."[10]

But here is Bunyan's great insight: sometimes we need a friend to help us turn the key. Why? Because God brings us hope through his Word, and his Word is external to us. We need to *hear* God's promises. The ideas swirling in our minds often seem hopeless. Even when we recall God's promises in our minds, we often do little more than weakly slip the key into the keyhole. We don't yet have the strength to turn it. But when a friend *speaks* these promises, when a friend brings this external Word to our ears, we gain strength to turn the key. It is as though our friend grabs the key with us and helps us to turn it.

Christian endured to the end, but only with the help of a friend.

My wife, Christina, just walked in from her night out, with a smile. Their conversation as friends covered the spectrum of heavy- to light-hearted. They shared their joys as well as their sorrows. Christina said, "It felt like true Christian fellowship— a lot of seriousness and a lot of laughter." She returned renewed by the presence and words of her friends.

3. COUNSEL FROM THE HEART

Third, friends help us figure out life in ways that no one else can. We all need wisdom. We get it from the Bible, from books, from professional counselors. We also get it from friends. Proverbs 27:9 says, "Oil and perfume make the heart glad, and the sweetness of a friend comes from his earnest counsel." This claims that one of the greatest joys of friendship is "earnest" counsel—literally, "counsel of soul," counsel from the heart. What fresh-baked chocolate chip cookies are to our sense of smell, a friend's counsel is to our soul. Close friends offer one another unique guidance because it comes from two things: personal knowledge and proven love.

First, close friends know us better than anyone else. In some ways, they may even know us better than we know ourselves. They see things about us that we don't see. They watch us rise and fall through joys and sorrows over the course of many years. They know how we think and what we value. They see how we respond to conflict and how we handle suffering. Their long history with us gives insight that a professional counselor cannot have. If each man and woman had a couple of true companions, friends who listened and loved well, then our world would need far fewer professional therapists.

Second, close friends love us more than any author or professional ever will. This is because they are personally invested in our decisions. What happens to us happens to them. Our problems are their problems. Our future is their future. They are bound to us in a way that others are not. So, while we rightly esteem the noble and necessary role of professional counselors, they should complement, not replace, the unique counsel of friends.

Several years ago I considered changing to a new job in a new place. So I brought my closest friends into the decision. In the end, of course, I bear responsibility for the choice. But it wasn't just my decision; it was *our* decision. Christina and I prayed for wisdom and looked for God to answer, in part, through our friends. We wanted the people closest to us to help us discern the wisest path forward. When we asked, "What do you think?" we weren't just looking for an opinion; we were asking them to help us make the decision. If nearly all of your wise friends agree about what you should do, you can make even the hardest decisions with settled confidence.

Sometimes we need friends to help us think a decision through. But other times we just need one to affirm that the decision we're making is reasonable. Sometimes we just need a friend to let us know we aren't crazy.

4. CHANGING THE WORLD THROUGH FRIENDSHIP

Fourth, friends strengthen our good resolves. Friendship is powerful. It is one of the greatest forces in the world. You may have an idea or a plan, and you may sense how you could accomplish it. But it may also sit in your mind like kindling that remains unlit. It often takes a friend to strike the match and then fan the flame with encouragement. Without friends, many of our resolutions would either never light up or quickly flicker out.

J. R. R. Tolkien emphasized this theme in *The Lord of the Rings*. Someone needs to carry the ring to the fires of Mordor. Frodo carries the ring, but he only accomplishes the mission because of his friends. In the middle of the journey, when one companion tries to steal the ring, Frodo abandons the fellowship. He no longer feels safe. But his closest friend, Sam, will not let him get away. As Frodo slips off across the river, Sam goes in after him. Frodo rejects his efforts at first: "I'm going to Mordor." But Sam replies, "Of course you are. And I'm coming with you."[11]

At that moment Sam knows better than Frodo what Frodo really needs. Frodo thanks him soon enough: "So all my plan is spoilt! . . . It is no good trying to escape you. . . . But I'm glad, Sam. I cannot tell you how glad. Come along!"[12] The two eventually finish the mission and save Middle Earth.

Without friendship, the ring never would have made it, and Middle Earth would have been destroyed. Actually, we never would have imagined Middle Earth in the first place because, without friendship, Tolkien never would have finished writing the story. He said that it was only C. S. Lewis's steady encouragement that kept him writing. Perhaps this is why the theme of friendship stands out so prominently in the story. In Tolkien's day, authors only produced "fairy stories" (as they were called) for children, not adults. But Tolkien wrote for adults too. He eventually wrote *The Lord of the Rings*, but it was only because of his relationship with Lewis. Two years after Lewis died, Tolkien reflected on Lewis's role in his life:

> The unpayable debt that I owe to him was not "influence" as it is ordinarily understood, but sheer encouragement. He was for long my only audience. Only from him did I ever get the idea that my "stuff" could be more than a private hobby. But for his interest and unceasing eagerness for more I should never have brought *the L. of the R.* to a conclusion.[13]

Lewis and Tolkien experienced true friendship. They knew that their experience was both wonderful and rare in their culture. This is why both men wrote to promote the joys of true friendship in their own day—Tolkien in *The Lord of the Rings*, and Lewis in *The Four Loves*.

One of the greatest gifts we can offer our friends is sheer encouragement. As we listen and light up to their ideas, we stir their souls into action. We lift their hearts and spur them on. Much of what is truly good in the world is the fruit of friendship.

5. WE MAKE FRIENDS AND THEN OUR FRIENDS MAKE US

Fifth, friends shape our character. We choose our friends, and then our friends shape who we become. In other words, at first we make our friends. From that point on, our friends make us. We can see this influence in three ways.

First, our friends *shape us.* They take the raw materials of our personality and influence the form they take. They shape us by drawing out parts of ourselves that would otherwise remain dormant. In this sense, our friends don't change us to become something else; they help us become who we truly are.

Yet each friend draws out only certain parts of our personality. Different friends water different seeds of our character. My friend Taylor waters different patches of my personality; Rick, Don, and Jeff water others. Friends cultivate the best or the worst in us, but either way, they bring out what is already there.

In other words, friendship reveals who we truly are. You cannot know yourself—not truly—without close relationships. If you don't have friends, much of who you are will remain hidden even to your own sight.

This explains why losing a friend feels like losing part of yourself. When one of your friends dies, part of you dies with him. That unique part will never come out in the same way again. When you bury a friend, you bury that part of your personality that only he brought out.

Second, our friends *influence the moral direction of our lives.* The ancient wisdom of Proverbs shows how this happens. Proverbs 13:20 says, "Whoever walks with the wise becomes wise, but the companion of fools will suffer harm." Similarly,

> Make no friendship with a man given to anger,
> > nor go with a wrathful man,
> lest you learn his ways
> > and entangle yourself in a snare. (Prov. 22:24–25)

Our friends show us our future selves. Friendship "makes good men better and bad men worse."[14] It also sometimes makes bad men better and good men worse. And the closer the friend, the stronger the influence.

This all happens much more subtly than we think. According to Proverbs, we don't just gain wisdom from *listening* to the instruction of the wise but by enjoying their friendship (13:20). The danger of spending time with an angry person is that we might "learn his ways" (22:24–25). This is not classroom, note-taking learning. It's far more subtle and far less intentional. Like a chameleon that changes colors when it lands on a branch, we become like those we spend time with.

How does this happen? Through the power of affections. We become like what we love. Since we love our friends, we increasingly love what they love. And then we inevitably live how they live. Character is contagious. This is why we must choose our friends wisely. Because we will inevitably become like them.

Third, friends also *make it easier to live a life of love.* We sacrifice for our friends, and we do it with ease. Friendship-love often feels effortless. We selflessly serve friends with a sense of of-course-ness. "It's nothing," we say. Even self-denial in friendship often doesn't feel much like self-denial. As Bertie Wooster put it, "When there is a chance of helping a pal we Woosters have no thought of self."[15]

Maybe you would like an example from an authority on this topic: Cookie Monster. With his friend standing beside him, he opened the jar and turned it upside down. One chocolate-chip cookie dropped onto the counter. He grabbed it and raised it toward his mouth. But then he glanced at his friend's pining eyes. So he paused to sing a song: "Sometimes me think, what is friend?" He explored this question in his song and then answered it most clearly at the end. Here's his profound conclusion: "Maybe friend somebody you give up last cookie for." Then, in a great moment of self-denial, he handed the cookie to his surprised companion. And when she offered to share the cookie with him, he insisted, "No, no, no, no, no. Friend eat cookie." He then looked to the camera and said, "Me feel strangely okay about this."[16]

This is perhaps Cookie Monster's most heroic act of self-sacrifice. But it doesn't feel like it to him. He shared his very last cookie, and yet he did it with a happy heart. That's the power of friendship. Friendship is a school of virtue, forming the habits of a life of love. That's what Cookie Monster shows us (though he may not put it quite like that).

As friendship transforms us in each of these ways, it also influences the rest of society around us. As we cultivate character in one another, we become not only better friends but better citizens. Personal relationships have public implications. Who we become in private always expresses itself in public. If we grow in empathy and kindness and selflessness among friends, we will demonstrate that in all our relationships. This is why one of the best ways to strengthen society is by filling it with overlapping networks of virtue-cultivating friendships.

6. FRIENDS MAKE FRIENDS LESS WEIRD

I end with one of friendship's most unsung benefits: friends make friends less weird. Without them, our world would be a much stranger place. This is because they iron out the more obnoxious wrinkles in our personality. A. C. Grayling put it best:

> If you think of someone who has no friends you see what can happen: a human being, like a neglected garden, may become rather overgrown—quite literally dirty and unkempt,

unsocial, introverted; after a bit, eccentric or half mad. Social intercourse keeps people—quite literally—clean and reasonably polite, sane and functional.[17]

Sometimes it takes a direct comment from a friend to change our behavior. But more often than not, it happens subtly and naturally. It happens without trying, or even thinking about it. Like stones in a river, the waters of friendship smooth us out over time. As we submerge ourselves into the lives of our friends, they each polish us and smooth over our jagged edges.

But even if oddities don't get ironed out, true friends still embrace and delight in them. Many of our friends' idiosyncrasies endear them to us. A friend's dramatic eyebrow raise, his occasional sense of obliviousness, her jarring laugh, his odd sense of humor. We should leave nearly every part of our friends untouched; it is no virtue to make every friend our twin. True friends embrace and learn to celebrate the uniqueness of their companions. They delight in one another's oddities.

And for those quirks of the less endearing type, Henry Ward Beecher's advice is best: "Every man should keep a fair-sized cemetery in which to bury the faults of his friends."

CONCLUSION

True friendship—not just relationships or community in general, but real and deep friendship—is one of life's greatest treasures. The six lost joys of real friendship unfolded above show us why friendship is worth all the effort we can muster. When we remember our highest highs and lowest lows in life, they often correspond with the presence or absence of our closest friends. Friends decrease every trouble and multiply every joy. Simply put, they make life better. Much better.

What, then, *is* true friendship?

QUESTIONS FOR REFLECTION AND DISCUSSION

1. Think back and identify the highest points of your life's journey. How often do you see friends present in your happiest memories? Would those moments be as happily remembered if friends weren't present?

2. Which friends of yours may be going through a difficult season of life? What are a few specific ways you can encourage them with your presence or words?

3. How have certain friends influenced your character for better? How have certain friends negatively influenced you?

4. Think about a few of your closest friends' interests and ambitions. Then think of one way you can encourage each friend to fulfill his or her good resolves.

4

A FRIEND WHO IS AS YOUR OWN SOUL

When thou hast found such a man, and proved the sincerity of his friendship; when he has been faithful . . . to thee, grapple him to thyself with hooks of steel and never let him go.

Charles Spurgeon

"A great thing is friendship," John Chrysostom preached, "and how great, no one can learn, and no discourse represent, but experience itself."[1] Our experiences of friendship shape our understanding of friendship. The friends we have influence what we think friendship means. This is why we might summarize our definition of friendship with the name of our closest friend. What is friendship? Dan. Joe. Jon.

But what if our experience falls short of true friendship and we don't even know it? What if we're missing something? How would we know? We may be like someone who thinks fast food is an ideal dinner only because he has never tasted steak. Many of us only know fast-food friendship. We have yet to experience filet mignon friendship.

This chapter describes ideal friendship so we know what to look for.

BOUND TOGETHER

Like love and beauty, friendship is hard to define. Proverbs distinguishes between "many companions" and "a friend who sticks closer than a brother" (Prov. 18:24). The difference here is not the kind of relationship but the degree of closeness.

We can place each of our relationships in concentric circles. Think of four rings, each one closer to the core (see Figure 1). These circles progress inward from impersonal relationships to acquaintances, to casual friends, to close friends. We'll see fewer people as we move to the center. Our closest friends cluster together in the tightest circle around us.

Relationships have also been described as lanes on a highway. Impersonal relationships drive along in the far right lane, the middle two lanes contain acquaintances and casual friends, and our closest friends travel with us in the left lane. A best friend or two may also ride in the car with us. The right lanes are full, and the left lanes have fewer people. Of course, blinkers flash and cars change lanes over time. A longtime acquaintance might later become a close friend. Or once-close friends may become little more than acquaintances. Perhaps a left-lane friend may swerve right to take the exit, later to re-enter and merge left again farther down the road.

Proverbs contrasts our many right-lane "companions" with a left-lane friend who "is closer than a brother." In this proverb's ancient context, family relationships were much closer than how we view them today. Family was seen as the tightest relational circle. Yet here a friend breaks inside that family circle and then moves even closer. Of course, a brother or sister could also become a close friend. This is true with my brother and me. Most siblings drive in the middle lanes, but Trent has become a left-lane friend to me. My brother became closer than a brother. We can say the same for marriage, which should be the closest friendship.[2] Christina knows me better than anyone else. She is my best friend. When couples recite their wedding vows, they are essentially promising lifelong, faithful friendship.

Figure 1

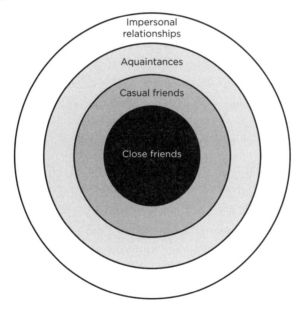

The Old Testament describes friendship with a striking phrase. Deuteronomy 13:6 refers to a close friend as one "who is as your own soul."[3] This suggests a deep oneness at the core of friendship. We see this at the beginning of David and Jonathan's relationship. Jonathan heard about David's faith through his courageous victory over Goliath. Very soon "the soul of Jonathan was knit to the soul of David" (1 Sam. 18:1). Like metals welded together, friendship is a binding of souls.[4] Two become bound up with and devoted to one another. This mysterious oneness lies at the heart of all true friendship.

We don't understand how this connection forms. It happened instantaneously with David and Jonathan. For others it develops over time. I experienced this instant bond with a few friends, but with others it took several years. I didn't think I would be close to some of them since we didn't connect well at first. But then, over time, we formed a lasting bond.

What is the essence of friendship? How do we define it? *Friendship is an affectionate bond forged between two people as they journey through life with openness and trust.*

THE MARKS OF TRUE FRIENDSHIP

What essential ingredients do we mix together to make true friendship? You won't find personality types on the list. Our extroversion or introversion will influence the flavor of our friendships, but neither personality type is better or worse. We don't need humor either, though I wouldn't want any of my friendships without a good dose of it. Also missing is anything to do with similarities in age, ethnicity, or social status. Whatever our differences, none of these necessarily keeps this deep bond from forming. Here are six essential ingredients of true friendship.

1. He Loved Him as His Own Soul

First, affection. One of the most common Hebrew words for friendship is *aheb*. It means "one who loves." Close friends hold each other in the highest esteem. They love each other.

We often experience the love of friendship as sheer enjoyment of one another. J. R. R. Tolkien underscores this in *The Lord of the Rings*. "Throughout their adventure the main benefit of their friendship is simply that they get to enjoy each other's company, to laugh and sing together, and to comfort and encourage each other."[5] In the previous chapter we read of C. S. Lewis's description of gathering with his friends. He most likely had Tolkien in mind as he wrote about those "golden sessions" when he and his friends gathered around a fire, "when the whole world, and something beyond the world, opens itself to our minds as we talk . . . at the same time an Affection mellowed by the years enfolds us."[6] True friends find themselves enfolded in an affection.

We also express our affection by renaming the people closest to us. Nicknames take a level of comfort for two people to give and receive. They convey a sense of belonging. The unique names we give demonstrate our affection. Of course, bullies give names to express belonging too, but they do it from a posture of superiority and ownership. True friends do it out of respectful and often playful endearment.

Among our closest relationships, this affection is sincere and heartfelt. We see this kind of love in Jonathan and David's friendship in the Old Testament. "Jonathan loved him as his own soul" (1 Sam. 18:1; see also v. 3).[7] He "delighted much in David" (19:1). At a crucial moment of testing in their relationship, "Jonathan made David swear again by his love for him, for he loved him as he loved his own soul" (20:17). When circumstances forced David away, they cried and kissed on the cheek

(20:41). And David was crushed in spirit when he heard about Jonathan's death, saying,

> I am distressed for you, my brother Jonathan;
>> very pleasant have you been to me;
> your love to me was extraordinary,
>> surpassing the love of women. (2 Sam. 1:26)

Family and friends have expressed affection this way throughout history. From the patriarch Joseph with his brothers to the apostle Paul with his companions, friends wept, embraced, and kissed as they parted (Gen. 45:14–15; Acts 20:37). These deep expressions of affection feel uncomfortable to us today. But C. S. Lewis observed, "On a broad historical view it is, of course, not the demonstrative gestures of friendship among our ancestors but the absence of such gestures in our own society that calls for some special explanation."[8] Jonathan and David model how to express strong affection and admiration between friends. Our generation needs to recapture something of this deeply felt and sincerely expressed bond of love.

2. Covenantal Friendship vs. Consumer Friendship

The second ingredient of true friendship is constancy. A real friend will never give you up or let you down. He will never turn away or desert you. Constant friends make the hard times easier and the easy times better. "A friend loves at all times," Proverbs says, "and a brother is born for adversity" (Prov. 17:17). And to paraphrase Proverbs 18:24, a man of many Facebook friends may come to ruin, but a true friend sticks closer than family.

Sometimes we view friendship as the one relationship without any commitment. We enter or exit at will. That's the beauty of it, right? Unlike marriage and family, we feel no obligation to stick it out. We freely give our loyalty as an ongoing choice.

It's true that we enter friendship voluntarily. But once we enter it, is it also true that we don't have any responsibilities to our friends? No. Everyone expects loyalty from friends. The Bible even commands it: when disaster strikes, "Do not forsake your friend or your father's friend" (Prov. 27:10).

All true friendship is, in a sense, covenantal. Jonathan and David explicitly made a covenant of friendship (1 Sam. 18:3). That covenant was not a mere legal contract. It made their commitments to one another explicit and permanent. It expressed and gave structure to their love.[9] David and Jonathan shared a deep commitment toward each other, and their covenant made that formal.

David drew on this covenant when his life was at risk. He said to Jonathan, "Deal kindly with your servant, for you have brought your servant into a covenant of the LORD with you" (20:8). "Deal kindly" translates the famous Hebrew word *hesed*. This is strong, covenantal language. *Hesed* means steadfast love. It takes our first two marks of friendship—affection and constancy—and packages them together in one word. God used it in Exodus 34:6 to declare his own constant love for his inconstant people. *Hesed* expresses God's deepest heart. David expected this from Jonathan.

Not every relationship needs a covenant. But even if we don't formalize our commitment, we still must make it felt. No friendship can last without loyalty.

If there is a code of friendship, it is surely this: "Never let a pal down."[10]

This covenantal friendship contrasts with consumer friendship. The consumer friend stays only as long as benefits remain. As soon as they disappear, so does the friend. Why? Because the consumer friend doesn't really want *you*; he only wants what you give. A consumer friend remains loyal only as long as his friend remains generous. As Proverbs says, "Wealth brings many new friends, but a poor man is deserted by his friend" (Prov. 19:4; cf. v. 6).

In contrast, a covenantal friend doesn't *use* you. He *enjoys* you.

Aelred of Rievaulx gives us wisdom here: once a friend proves faithful, "that friend is to be so tolerated, so treated, and so encouraged that as long as he does not depart irrevocably from the foundation you have built, he should be so much yours and you so much his . . . that there should exist no separation of spirits, affection, will, or opinion."[11] In other words, a constant friend deserves a constant friend in return.

Suffering is the great relationship revealer. We often learn how strong a friendship is when we don't have anything to give. We also find out what kind of friends *we* are when a friend can't give anything to *us*. When someone cannot share anything but a burden, only covenantal friends stick around to carry it. I think of my grandfather's friendships formed through serving in World War II. The trials they shared in battle forged deep bonds between them. Every one of them would have given his life for the others, and every one of them knew it. This is why a few of the men he served with in his twenties remained close friends through his seventies. They stayed together because they suffered together.

We see this same resolve in the biblical story of Ruth. Naomi grieved the death of her husband and two sons. She came to Moab full, and she left empty. Yet not entirely, because she gained a friend. Ruth, her daughter-in-law, stuck with her: "Where you go I will go, and where you lodge I will lodge. Your people shall be my people, and your God my God. Where you die I will die, and there will I be buried. May the LORD do so to me and more also if anything but death parts me from you" (Ruth 1:16–17). Strong statements. We hear a covenantal ring in them, which is why people often quote them in marriage ceremonies. There was no use trying to escape Ruth's tenacity. And Naomi wouldn't want to. She had nothing to offer Ruth, but Ruth clung to her for two reasons: Naomi's God was her God. And Naomi was her friend.

Of course, constancy is hard. Time passes, and we realize six months have passed since we last contacted our friend. We know delaying will only make it worse, and yet, inexplicably, we still don't call! We feel guilty and sheepish, especially when we've also forgotten to return our friend's calls. But that's okay. Sometimes constancy sounds like a sincere apology for *not* being constant. When we apologize, a true friend will receive that. We will both move forward from there, picking up where we left off, happy to reconnect. The friendship grows stronger, not weaker, for these times of reconciliation. Constant friendships weather inconstancies with grace.

What does it look like when someone plods through decades with this kind of constancy? It reminds me of one of my favorite pictures of my grandfather, Fred. He and his best friend, Paul, were in their seventies at the time. They have their arms open and their faces are lit up as they greet each other with a hug. They had been friends since childhood, and they remained close to each other for their entire lives. And it was a functional friendship too—they didn't just stay in touch, they often spent time together.

3. Giving a Clear View

The third mark is transparency. We know friendship requires honesty. But we also know how to be honest without being open. Real friends don't just know the truth about each other; they know the whole truth. They sometimes see us more clearly than we even see ourselves.

As light shines through transparent objects, real friends can see into our souls. Over time, our friends learn our greatest joys and deepest sorrows. They learn our strongest beliefs, opinions, and fears. They know our most challenging temptations and our most shameful failures. We crack open the doors of our souls to our friends. And when we don't, our friends gently knock because they care enough to see how we're really doing inside. Every one of us needs at least one person who knows us as well as we know ourselves, perhaps even better than we know ourselves.

True friends walk in the light together. The apostle John writes, "If we walk in the light, as he is in the light, we have fellowship with one another, and the blood of Jesus his Son cleanses us from all sin" (1 John 1:7). What does it mean to walk in the light? I used to think it only referred to obedience. But notice: the light is the place of cleansing. This means that darkness isn't just the place where we disobey; it's the place were we hide. And the light isn't just where we obey, but where we *come out of hiding*, where we open up about how we've *dis*obeyed.

Walking in the light, then, isn't about being perfect; it's about admitting we're not.

As we confess our sins to God and others, we find real forgiveness and true fellowship (1:6–7). This is because God's grace doesn't just cleanse us but creates an atmosphere of safety among fellow sinners. If God loved us while we were still sinners, and if he *still* loves us while we *are still* sinners, then we can be honest about who we really are. When we open up to trusted friends, and they don't shrink back but move closer, that's when friendship gets traction.

Honesty + Acceptance = Real Friendship

4. The Rarest Jewel in Friendship

Fourth, candor. True friends speak with straightforward honesty. The English Puritan Thomas Goodwin wrote, "Simplicity and plain-heartedness . . . is the truest and rarest jewel in friendship."[12]

We speak clearly but also gently. Because we're speaking with our *friend*.

Sometimes, and only when necessary, this means delivering hard words. We all need correction from time to time. The best people to give it are our closest friends. Proverbs 27:5–6 says,

> Better is open rebuke
> than hidden love.
> Faithful are the wounds of a friend;
> profuse are the kisses of an enemy.

A good friend loves enough to give these faithful wounds, and also loves enough to do it kindly.

When you rebuke others, you are telling them that they have a problem. But what is rebuke, more deeply? If it contrasts with "hidden love," then it must be public love. Here's what that means: If someone I love is heading into foolishness, and I refuse to tell him, I'm *hiding* love. I'm holding it back. Why would I do that? Perhaps I care more about what my friend thinks *about* me than I care about what he needs *from* me. Yet when we withhold a necessary rebuke, it's like hiding critical medicine from a sick friend.

When we administer this medicine of rebuke, we should use caution. Rebuke is potent medication, but too much proves lethal. If you give a lot of criticism, you probably give too much.

We honor our friends when we make affirmation the norm, not critique. Wisely placed criticism lands softly on the padding of several dozen encouragements laid down in previous months. A friendship filled with affirmation helps it to absorb occasional correction. This is one reason why friendship is an ideal context for correction. The broader context of our relationship together minimizes the confrontational element of rebuke. We help our friends with helpful correction in the context of ordinary life.

Rebuke is risky. We wonder how our friend will respond. Do we risk beginning a hard conversation by speaking directly, or do we stay silent to maintain peace? If we speak, we create a moment of testing: Will our friend understand that we're rebuking out of love, or will he think we're attacking him? One friend of mine told me that she addressed a serious sin in her friend's life, but her friend was unwilling to repent. Her friend resented her for bringing it up, and their friendship ended. Rebuke is risky because someone may respond to our correction by swerving across a couple of lanes to take the nearest exit. On the other hand, our friend may thank us and move even closer.

Of course, when it's our time to receive the wound, let's receive it well. Our friends feel as much pain by giving the rebuke as we do in receiving it, like a mother wincing as she removes the sliver from her toddler's foot. They also do it with the anxious uncertainty of wondering how we will respond. We need to remember, therefore, that when friends tell us our faults, they are as Charles Spurgeon put it "performing on [our] behalf the most heroic act of pure charity."[13] Who wouldn't want a friend like that?

So, in these turbulent moments, we need to remember above all else that our friend is . . . our *friend*. She works as a soul doctor, hurting only to help. She deserves the honor of our gratitude.

5. Seeing through Their Eyes

Empathy, the fifth mark of friendship, is the ability to understand and adjust to someone's emotional state. It is the capacity to enter his mind, to peer out at the world through his eyes. Empathetic friends weep with friends who weep and rejoice with friends who rejoice. We understand how they feel and why they feel it. And we also feel it with them.

Empathy shapes the whole tone of a relationship. Without it, we trade honoring friends for one-upping them. We trade affirmation for sarcasm. We trade talking *with* for talking *at*. We trade listening to sorrows for changing the subject.

Over time we learn our friends' temperaments, their moods, and their buttons. We know what makes them tick and what ticks them off. This all informs how we relate to them. We pick up on our friend's emotional state and we adapt to it. As we do this, consideration serves as a primary way that we bear our friend's burdens. An empathetic presence lightens our friend's load. Troubles drop down like Tetris blocks. Some of them pile up on our friend's back. But one well-placed, empathetic word can slide in and clear half the load.

Sometimes this means, quite literally, weeping with those who weep. My wife and I lost our first child, Hope, in pregnancy. We stayed home for several days to talk, read, pray, and cry. Many people comforted us. But a few comments stand out. Some people made well-meaning but strikingly inconsiderate remarks. "What do you think you did wrong?" "I'm sure you'll have another one soon." But two friends stand out because of how their comments reduced the burden that pressed down on my back. First, when I told my brother about our baby's passing, he just cried. And then he prayed for us. This still moves me to tears today. Second, when I told another friend what happened, he paused, looked across the table at me, and asked if anyone had made any insensitive comments. He wisely understood that part of the burden my wife and I carried was the loneliness of not being understood. My friends' empathy slid into place and cleared a big part of our load that difficult week.

6. The Foundation of Friendship

The sixth mark of friendship is trust. True friends keep confidences.

We learn the importance of trust when it's not there. One of the characters in the book of Proverbs is "the whisperer." Proverbs 16:28 says, "A dishonest man spreads strife, and a whisperer separates close friends." Proverbs 17:9 says, "Whoever covers an offense seeks love, but he who repeats a matter separates close friends." The whisperer shares information, whether true or false, that should stay hidden. He wraps it up, labels it as a "concern" or a "prayer request," and delivers it to whomever will hear.

Proverbs says *beware!* because this severs even the closest relationships. Gossip erodes trust, and distrust erodes friendship. It is the opposite of safety. If you suspect that someone may talk about your issues behind your back, you won't share them anymore. You won't open up. Suspicion will tint your lenses when you look at your friend. It will shade how you see every aspect of the relationship. When distrust enters your relationship, you may remain friendly, but you can't remain real friends.

I know what it's like to have false rumors spread about me. I didn't know who started them. I didn't know who heard them.

And worse, I didn't know who *believed* them. The rumors misrepresented my actions, and more deeply, they struck at my character. Very quickly, I wasn't sure who to trust.

But that situation taught me the nature of real trust. Trust shone forth in friends who didn't even have to ask me if the rumors they heard were true. They dismissed them out of hand.

Maybe you've heard about someone "whispering" things about you too. When a friend breaks confidence with you, the relationship becomes like a house with a cracked foundation. A big enough gap compromises the integrity of the whole structure. We can't live in a trustless relationship any longer than we can live in a shifting house. A suspicious friendship isn't sustainable because it isn't safe. If a foundation has enough problems, we either fix it or move out.

NOT GUARANTEES

These six ingredients of friendship are not guarantees. We may embody them all yet still lack even one real friend.

This is because friends need to reciprocate these marks. We may want someone to be our friend. We may show them affection, constancy, empathy, and so forth. But if this friend does not share the desire for friendship, it won't happen. If I flick on my left blinker to shift into someone's lane, they may not slow down to make space for me. I may even think I'm cruising along in someone's casual-friend middle lane, but he may think of me as driving out on the service road. Friendship requires mutuality—mutual affection, mutual constancy, and so forth.

Yet even with reciprocation, we still can't force the bond to forge. Even if I experience all of these marks with someone, this does not guarantee that our relationship will be particularly close. We can create the best conditions for friendship by pursuing these marks, but we cannot force it. We can't manipulate the binding of souls.

These marks also don't guarantee that our friendships will be healthy or beneficial. None of the marks alone, nor all of them together, mean that our friendships will help us become better people. These characterize *deep* friendship but not necessarily *good* friendship. Bullies have their friends too, but that doesn't make the playground any safer.

A DEEPER BOND AND A DISTANT HORIZON

In addition to the six marks, C. S. Lewis observed that friendships are always "about something."[14] Some friends unite in their enthusiasm for basketball. Some share an interest in literature or poetry. Some share a commitment to running or biking or weight lifting.

Christians share common interests with friends as well, but they also unite around the most important thing about them. Friendships are always "about something," and Christian friendship is, at its core, about Jesus Christ. When we become Christians, we're not just about some*thing* but some*one*. This is true Christian friendship—what others in times past referred to as *spiritual friendship*. Spiritual friendship places Christ at the center and pursues Christlikeness as the goal. In other words, in spiritual friendship, we always include Jesus as our third Friend.

As Thomas Brooks encourages us, "Let those be your choicest companions who have made Christ their chief companion."[15]

When Christ serves as the glue of our relationships, we find that we bond together with people who are otherwise very different from us. As individuals and as churches, we should eagerly celebrate diversity—diversity of races, ages, and backgrounds.

Every friendship also has a horizon—a shared direction toward which it moves. Friends unite together in a "common quest or vision" in life.[16] We're all on a journey somewhere, and our friends are those who travel with us. We walk along life's path toward a shared horizon, and Christians look out to a horizon that extends even farther ahead. We're on a journey together, and the horizon stretches onward forever.

The New Testament calls Christians to lift their eyes to "the Day," the day of Jesus's return (Heb. 10:25). This is the horizon above and beyond all horizons. This shapes the focus of Christian relationships. We "exhort one another every day" (Heb. 3:12) and "consider how to stir up one another to love and good works . . . encouraging one another, and all the more as you see the Day drawing near" (10:24–25). In context, these are directions for an entire church community. But how does this get worked out in practice? It gets worked out in friendship. We can't experience this everyday encouragement with every person in our church. This command gets traction as we carry it out in smaller networks of relationships—in friendships. In other words, perseverance in the faith requires the practice of friendship.

This means that we should view discipleship as a form of friendship. Real discipleship—helping others follow Jesus—happens in the rhythms of everyday life. Discipleship works best when we pursue it in life-on-life relationships. As we ride in the car together, we ask our friend how his relationship with God is going. When we grab a meal together, we hear about a struggle we can pray about together. When we do an activity, we ask what she's encouraged about from God's Word. In these ordinary ways we help one another follow Jesus.

We mature as Christians as we enjoy biblical friendship with discipleship intentionality.

CONCLUSION

These essential marks, with this deeper bond and horizon in Christ, create relationships that are less like fast food and more like filet mignon. Friendship is an affectionate bond that deepens between two people as they travel toward the day of Christ with openness and trust.

But how do we get there? As we think about these marks, we may realize just how little we really experience true friendship. This chapter shows us the target out there in the distance, and now we see all our arrows scattered on the ground, depressingly close to where we launched them. That's how I often feel. Some of us have many rich friendships. Some of us have none. Maybe you thought you had deep friendships, but now you see that you've only known casual companionship. So, how do we launch our arrows so that they lodge in the target?

We need practical wisdom. That's where we'll turn next.

QUESTIONS FOR REFLECTION AND DISCUSSION

1. Which ingredient of friendship is most rare in friendships today? Why do you think that is the case?

2. Which essential mark do you lack most in your friendships? What has kept you from growing in this?

3. Who in your life most closely fits this chapter's description of true friendship? What characteristics make him or her a good friend?

4. Take a few minutes to thoughtfully identify in which lane the people closest to you drive. Who would you identify as your closest friends? Who are your casual friends? Who are a few of the people more accurately identified as acquaintances than friends?

5. What are your closest friendships "about"? What are two things you can do to encourage one another in growing as disciples of Jesus as you look to the horizon of his return?

5

CULTIVATING FRIENDSHIP

We have few friendships, because we are not willing to pay the price of friendship. . . . The secret of
friendship is just the secret of all spiritual blessing.
The way to get is to give.

Hugh Black

Here's a myth about friendship: it just happens. I used to believe that. I didn't think it required skill, effort, or careful
work. But I've learned that friendships—*good* friendships—
require cultivation.

We can think of cultivating friendships like cultivating the
ground. When my family and I moved to Indiana a few years
ago, we found many people who planted gardens in their yards.
So we tried it too. The first year we planted too much, too close
together, and with too little understanding of how to maintain it.
Since I neglected the cucumbers (which were my only responsibility), they sprawled out like a wild vine over the whole garden

bed. We tried again the next year but made the garden one-third smaller. This time weeds took over and nearly choked everything else out. This past spring we considered filling it all in with grass. But we decided to try again. And it's working out this time.

Why? We're learning to cultivate. Specifically, we now have wisdom, we put in the work, and we uproot weeds. Because we lacked these three things before, our garden turned into a wasteland and we almost gave up. But now we watch our kids happily gather up raspberries, tomatoes, and cucumbers.

Similarly, without cultivation, friendships either wither or become unruly. Sometimes we may even feel like giving up. If you're like me, the last chapter made you realize that you're not as good a friend as you thought. Or maybe you've enjoyed friendships, but you want to be a better friend. Where do we go from here? How do we cultivate better friendships?

True friendships take *wisdom*, they take *work*, and, in a fallen world, they take *weeding*. They are also worth every bit of the effort we put into them.

PRACTICING WISDOM

Wisdom is about living well in the world. We grow in wisdom as we see how God designed life to work, and then we adjust to fit with that design. God made different relationships to work in different ways. Marriage, parenting, and work relationships each require different approaches. Like these relationships, friendships flourish when we approach them with certain principles in mind. Let's consider four of them.

Give Your Friends a Promotion

When friendships fail, we can usually trace it back to imbalanced priorities. We rightly value things such as work, family, and rest. But if we let any or all of those fill our lives, we won't have any room left for friends.

One myth that keeps us from enjoying friendship is that we're too busy for it. It may be true that you *are* too busy for friends. But that doesn't mean you *should* be. We always make time for what we treasure. Consider how much time you spend each week on personal entertainment such as watching sports and shows or clicking through social media. Could you trade some of those hours for time with a friend? Our lives may seem busy, but if we promote our friends in our priorities, we will find space for them in our schedules. This will often involve sacrifice. We will have to say no to other good things in order to say yes to our friends.

What do we do if we have to move away from friends? First, keep strengthening your longtime friendships. We don't need to end our relationships when we move away. We can stay in touch through calls and letters and messages, and we can plan to travel to meet up together.

Second, invest in forming new relationships where you live. We may not proactively make friends in a new area because we fear that we won't find any. Or we may resist making new friends because we aren't certain how long we'll stay here. But consider what my friends Scott and Katie did. They were moving from California to Illinois for Scott to start graduate school. They cried on the way because they were leaving their closest friends. They would only be in Illinois for two years, but on that drive they made a decision: they committed to make sure that it would hurt just as much to move *away from* Illinois as it did to move *to* Illinois.

Third, maybe you don't have to move. C. S. Lewis wrote to his friend, "If I had to give a piece of advice to a young man about a place to live, I think I should say, 'sacrifice almost everything to live where you can be near your friends.' I know I am very fortunate in that respect."[1] That may not sound realistic for most of us most of the time. We're often forced to move due to family needs or work changes. But if friendship really is as great as Lewis and others say it is, then shouldn't it at least factor into the decision? Maybe we should sometimes turn down a bigger paycheck if it means we have to move away from the people who contribute so much joy to our lives and in whom we've invested so much time and effort.

Take a Dose of Realism

Here's another myth about friendship: we can have a lot of very close friends. If friendship takes time, and we only have so much of it, then we won't have enough to share with everyone. This shouldn't discourage us; it just means that good friends are like the best meals. A Thanksgiving spread looks great, but you can only fit so much on one plate.

If we try to collect too many close friends, we'll end up with no close friends at all. When I planted too much too close together, my whole garden turned into an unruly wasteland. In a similar way, we can't be too close to too many people—not because it's wrong, but because it's unrealistic. As the English proverb puts it, "A friend to all is a friend to none."

Many people whom we call friends, or whom we "friend" on Facebook, are more accurately called acquaintances or connections. We shouldn't feel bad about having a limited number of deep relationships. One way for us to recover true friendship in our day is to simultaneously recover the value of acquaintanceship.[2] Certain people we know and spend time with are our acquaintances, and that's a good thing. We shouldn't feel bad for being unable to draw everyone into our closest circle of relationships. We can appreciate everyone in our lives, yet the sacred bonds of friendship will only form with a small percentage of them.

You Don't Make Vows, But . . .

Does friendship come with responsibility? We may not have thought much about friendship entailing commitments, but we all know that it does. We imply it when we say, "I thought we were friends." Or when we think, *I could never do that to my friend*. We sense it in David's lament in the Psalms,

> For it is not an enemy who taunts me—
> > then I could bear it;
> it is not an adversary who deals insolently with me . . .
> But it is you, a man, my equal,
> > my companion, my familiar friend. (Ps. 55:12–13)

Esther Edwards Burr expressed her commitment to friendship in a journal entry from 1756: "I look on the ties of friendship as sacred . . . it ought to be a matter of solemn prayer to God; where there is a friendship [begun] that it may be preserved."[3] We don't slide friendship rings onto our fingers. Obligations don't bind us in the same way as marriage vows. Nevertheless, as Burr said, the bonds of friendship are *sacred*. A friend must be "treated as a friend deserves."[4]

Think about your closest friends. How should you treat them if it's true that you really are tied together with a sacred knot?

Realign Your Expectations

Friendship also requires flexibility. In the last chapter I used the illustration of "relationship lanes" on a highway to describe the relative closeness of the people in our lives. You may consider Dave a close friend who travels with you in your left lane. But then you realize that he doesn't see it this way. You're the one initiating all of the conversations. You expect him to spend a lot of time with you, but he expects much less. He's *your* close friend, but you're not *his*. What do you do? His view of you may change over time, but you have to adjust your expectations for now. If he pictures you in his middle lane, you may need to start picturing yourself that way too. Otherwise, if you force your friends to adjust to your expectations, they may take the next exit.

Or what if you don't think you're very close to Dave, but you learn that you're one of his closest friends? You don't have to adjust to him. But you can. I did this with someone a few years ago. When I realized he viewed me as one of his closest friends, I felt bad for him at first because it wasn't mutual. But then, after a few moments of thinking about it, I felt honored. I was grateful that he considered me so close to him. So I adjusted my opinions about our friendship, and we're now close friends.

Many friendships also change over time. Sometimes friends change lanes. People move from the left lane to a middle lane, or from a right lane to an exit. This doesn't contradict the previous principle—that friendship entails commitment. It means that we don't require every friendship to last a lifetime. If friendships weren't fluid, we would each stay locked into the three closest friends we made on the fourth-grade playground.

PUTTING IN THE WORK

It's true that friendships often begin without effort. But that's not how friendships endure. Starting a marathon doesn't take work, but finishing it does. After thinking about friendship through his life, my dad said, "I know one thing—for two people to be true friends, it takes work and sacrifice." Relationships thrive when we're intentional about friendships in four simple ways.

Talking Face to Face

First, friendships flourish when we talk together, especially face to face. One of the best gifts life offers us is unhurried conversation with close friends. Thomas Goodwin put it this way: "Mutual communion is the soul of all true friendship; and familiar conversation with a friend has the greatest sweetness in it."[5]

Some ways of communicating strengthen friendship better than others. When we send digital messages, we're most often sustaining, rather than deepening, our friendships. Phone calls move us a bit closer because they allow more of our personality, more of who we are, to come through. Best, of course, are face-to-face and eye-to-eye conversations.

When the apostle John wrote to his friends, he wished that he didn't have to. "Though I have much to write to you," he wrote, "I would rather not use paper and ink. Instead I hope to come to you and talk face to face, so that our joy may be complete" (2 John 12; see 3 John 13–14). He wrote, but he preferred to look them in the eyes. John Calvin said about his friend, "If only he lived close by. A three-hour talk would exceed a hundred letters."[6]

Nothing replaces the value of embodied conversation, yet messages, letters, and phone calls keep us in touch with distant friends. My brother Trent and I live in different states, and we only see one another a couple of times every year. We mainly keep up through talking on the phone a couple of times each week. If something really big happens to one of us, we pick up the phone. If one of us has a particularly hard couple of days, we pick up the phone. He would be dumbfounded if he first heard about a big life change from someone else instead of from me.

But talking openly is even more important than talking often.

Every one of us should have a few trusted confidants to whom we've granted full access to the full truth about us. Here's what I mean: Each of us is like a lake, with both shallow areas and hidden depths. We can open the shallows to public fishing. But we should also have a few trusted friends who can access the deeper parts. We explain to them the terrain, and we give them a license to fish there.

The best conversations happen when both friends ask thoughtful and personal questions. Conversations drain us when one person is either too dominant (always talking but never listening) or too passive (always listening but never contributing). Both approaches—yammering on or never engaging—reveal a lack of love. If you're always active in conversation, but you only share interesting (or uninteresting) details about your life, you won't have deep friendships. If you're always passive, and you never ask about anyone else's life, you won't have deep friendships. Conversation thrives with the give and take of two practices: engaged listening and measured speaking.

Of course, true friendship isn't entirely or even most often serious. In my closest friendships we pour in a good dose of levity with the gravity. If no one would laugh when they overheard some of my conversations with friends, I figure we're not doing it right.

How can each of us deepen our conversations in friendship? Here are a few practical ideas:

Getting Practical

- Think about what to ask people when you're on your way to meet with them. What do you want to find out about? How can you encourage them?
- Grab a meal or coffee with someone. Schedule this time together monthly or every other week. Consider discussing the Bible or a book together when you meet.
- Talk about spiritually significant topics. Ask what your friend is reading in the Bible or in a good book recently. Ask how they are encouraged or discouraged in their life of faith right now. (If you aren't in the habit of having these types of conversations, it might feel awkward at first. Do it anyway, perhaps acknowledging to your friend that it may feel awkward.)
- Let a couple of close friends know they can correct you when they think it best, and then you promise to receive it well.
- Use your drive home from school or work or the store to catch up with a distant friend. Even if you only have three minutes. And if you don't reach them, leave an encouraging voicemail.
- Add four or five friends to your phone's speed dial list so that you can call them more easily more often.
- Think about someone to whom you often write messages, emails, or letters. Instead of writing, ask them to get together or, if they're far away, call them.

Doing Things Side by Side

Second, friendships feed on shared experience—life on life and side by side. Near the end of his life, the author John Stott was asked, "When do you feel most alive?" How would you answer that? Here are the three things that made him feel most alive:

public worship, enjoying nature, and human friendships. "I'm grateful to have many friends," he said, "and very grateful to have the opportunity to enjoy their friendship, and to do things with them."[7] I love how he expressed it so plainly: "and to do things with them." A large part of friendship consists of simply doing things together.

Of course, in order to "do things" together, we have to *be* together. But how do we make space in our full schedules? Sometimes we don't have to. We can invite friends into what we already do. I usually tune into NBA games once playoff season comes around. Rather than watching alone, I invite friends over to watch the game together. What shows do you watch? Do you go for walks? When do you go to the store? Invite a friend into these activities.

The best way to create space for closer relationships is to establish rhythms. Much of the time I spend with friends happens as part of a rhythm in my schedule. Taylor and I grab coffee every other Tuesday after work. My wife and I invite people over for dinner or dessert on Wednesdays. Each July I take an extended weekend to go on an outdoor adventure with longtime friends. Every three or four months I get together for an evening with three friends who live a few hours away.

Find your own friendship rhythms. Establish rails for your relationships to ride along over the long haul.

What about when it's too hard to establish a rhythm of getting together? In these cases, friendship also grows from spontaneity mixed with sacrifice. That's what my friend Jonny showed me a few years ago. He had Labor Day weekend open, and the thought flitted into his mind to visit me. But he lives in Maryland and I live in Indiana so, after looking up the distance, he said to his dad, "I was going to visit my buddy, but then I saw he was *eleven* hours away." His dad replied, "And *why* aren't you going?" Jonny thought for a few seconds. "I'm not really sure. . . . I guess I'll go."

Friends do things together. It's not complicated. And the best part of friendship is not the *doing* but the *being*. When you're with good friends, just being together is more important than whatever it is you're doing.

Getting Practical

- If you plan to watch a movie or sports, invite a friend over to join you. Save a certain show for watching with a friend or in a group.
- With the next book you plan to read, invite one or more people to read it and to meet a few times along the way for discussion.
- If you're a parent with young children at home, invite someone to join you on a walk or a visit to a park.
- Ask a friend to help you with a home-improvement project, or offer to help your friends with theirs.
- Regularly exercise, work out, or play a sport with someone.
- Ask a friend to go on a walk together. Make it a weekly or every-other-week rhythm.
- Develop your own annual traditions of camping, heading to a city with friends, or enjoying a concert.
- If you're married, make a plan with your spouse for how to help each other cultivate friendships. Create space for one another to do this. Encourage one another in it.

Eating around the Table

Friendships thrive when we eat together. Throughout history and the world, wherever we find strong community, we also find shared meals at the center of it. Why? Because one of the main reasons meals exist is to enrich relationships.

A central theme in the Bible is that of a joyful feast in God's presence. God's first command to Adam was to eat from all of Eden's trees (Gen. 2:17). In the Old Testament, people also typically ate together when making a covenant. After Israel's exodus from Egypt, their leaders climbed Mount Sinai and "they beheld God, and ate and drank" (Ex. 24:11). Then God brought Israel into their land and commanded them to rejoice (*commanded* to rejoice!) over meals in his presence (Deut. 12:18; 14:26; 27:7). Then Jesus "came eating and drinking" (Matt. 11:19), and he enlivened a wedding feast with wine as the first sign of the breaking in of the new creation (John 2:1–11). Then on the night before he died, he left his disciples with a meal of remembrance (Luke 22:15–16). And when he returns, he will bring this age to its conclusion with the joyful laughter of a wedding feast (Rev. 19:7–9).

What's with all the food?

Friendship.

Food changes things. The first year I led a small group of college students, we met in the library of our church's building. Everyone typically showed up late and left early. They said they had too much homework to do. But then we started meeting in my home, and we ate dinner together as the first part of our meeting. People started to come early and stay late, even with the same amount of homework. What changed? A meal around a table. Instead of rushing into our discussion, we first enjoyed talking around the table (or on the couch or the floor or wherever people found a place to sit).

Every one of us eats about twenty-one meals each week. Why not share a few of these with friends? Make this one of your relational rhythms. One man I know meets with friends for breakfast every three or four weeks, and they've been at it for forty-eight years.

Getting Practical

- Pick one breakfast slot each week and invite a different friend to join you each time.
- As you leave your church's Sunday service, invite someone out or over to your home for lunch. Talk about what convicted or encouraged you from the sermon.
- Keep one evening open each week to invite someone over for dinner.
- If you have younger children, invite someone over for dessert after your children go to bed. Or invite a friend to join the dinnertime fun and to stick around for family Bible reading and prayer.
- If you're part of a small group or study group, add a pitch-in dinner to your meetings.

Encouraging from the Heart

Encouragement is relational oxygen. If you've ever hiked at a high altitude, you know that it gets hard to breathe. When the air thins out, a little effort takes a lot out of you. You feel more sluggish more quickly. That's how every relationship feels in the absence of much affirmation and encouragement. But when we encourage one another, it's like thickening the air with oxygen.

As oxygen is to our lungs, encouragement is to our souls.

Oxygen gives life. Remove it, and we die. Proverbs says, "Death and life are in the power of the tongue" (Prov. 18:21). When the atmosphere is thick with affirmation, friendships thrive. But when it's thin (or when it's thick with criticism), they wither.

My friend Dane often calls to talk for just a few minutes. He rarely calls with any reason other than to check in. And before the conversation ends, he often shares a couple of reasons why he thanks God for me. My friend Bill does this too. He sent me a note one Saturday night because he knew I would be teaching the next morning. He wrote, "You are all prayed up for the service and your teaching. So proud of you, you ol' booger." Sincerity with levity. He sent these messages at other times: "You and Christina are treasured friends." "We love and appreciate both of you." "I continue to be so thankful for our friendship." *Oxygen*.

These friends remind me of the apostle Paul. I often think of Paul as an evangelist or a theologian. But he also lived as a man of friendship, and he filled the atmosphere of his relationships with affirmation. Sometimes he adds a final section of greetings at the end of his letters. He often adds personal side comments to the names he lists. For example, at the end of Romans, Paul greets twenty-eight people by name. He thanks Prisca and Aquila, who "risked their necks for my life" (16:3); he calls Phoebe a servant (v. 1), Mary and Persis hard workers (vv. 6, 12), and Apelles approved in Christ (v. 10); he calls four of them "beloved." What's with all the public affirmation? Oxygen.

Maybe it doesn't feel normal to look your friend in the eye and say why you respect him or her. But it should. Whenever something feels upside down, we might ask: Is *this* upside down, or am *I*? Affirmation will feel out of place in a relational culture where sarcasm, competition, and comparison are the norm.

But what does it feel like when encouraging words replace those? It feels like a church I visited a few years ago. Affirmation was a palpable part of the culture. Romans 12:10 marked their relational tone: "Love one another with brotherly affection. Outdo one another in showing honor." I asked one of the men there what he thought about this. He told me that when he first showed up, it felt awkward. He never had men look him in the eye and tell him why they appreciated him, why they respected him. But he said that over the course of a few months he changed; he said it was as if he was being rewired. He realized that *he* had been upside down, and that he was made for this kind of culture. We all were.

Affirming others will initially feel uncomfortable if you aren't used to it. But the more you encourage, the less strange it will feel. Over time, it may sufficiently change the relational culture around you so that it won't feel awkward anymore.

One of the best ways we can encourage friends is through written notes. I have several notes saved in a drawer that I've pulled out to re-read for encouragement. I have a file on my computer for particularly thoughtful and kind notes. I know others who do this as well, and they find ongoing encouragement from re-reading them over time.

Getting Practical

- Here's a principle to live by: whenever the thought crosses your mind to affirm something about someone, do it, and do it without hesitation.
- Sometimes, before you say goodbye to friends, say why you're thankful for them. Let them know you love them and that you thank God for them.
- When you mention people's names in conversation, create the habit of adding a comment about why you respect them.
- On a friend's birthday, write a thoughtful and encouraging letter to them to let them know why you respect and admire them.

Each of these practices—talking, doing, eating, and encouraging—takes work. The two best ways to integrate these into our lives is with rhythms and creativity.

First, with rhythms, we turn these ideas into practice. We lay down rails in our schedules for our friendships to ride along. When we set patterns in our lives, we no longer rely on our whims; we build them into our schedules because they're important. And even with these rhythms, we still need to stay flexible. When life changes, our rhythms also need to change. If the season of your life changes, change your friendship rhythms to fit the new season.

Second, creativity keeps things personal and fresh. Perhaps many of the practical suggestions above don't work for you. Maybe some don't fit with your personality. That's fine. Think of creative approaches that work for you.

PULLING WEEDS

I spent a couple of summers working with a landscaping crew. We planted bushes, spread mulch, and mowed lawns. We also pulled *a lot* of weeds. I often thought about Genesis 3:17–18: "Cursed is the ground because of you; . . . thorns and thistles it shall bring forth for you." Just as prickly weeds cover the ground, relational weeds infest our friendships. Cultivating true friendship entails pulling these weeds up by the roots. The sages who wrote Proverbs warn us to look out for three of them.

1. When Your Blessing Sounds Like Cursing

First, beware of inconsiderateness. Proverbs compares singing songs to a heavy heart with taking someone's coat when it's cold (Prov. 25:20). When someone weeps with sorrow, our cheery smiles do not relieve but add to their burden. Proverbs also warns,

Whoever blesses his neighbor with a loud voice,
　　rising early in the morning,
　　will be counted as cursing. (27:14)

Friendly greetings are nice. But too much too loud, and before our friend has coffee, is rude. In each of these cases, these aren't the actions of a bully; they are the thoughtless missteps of an inconsiderate friend. These are fine gestures, but they have bad timing. We think we're handing our friend a flower, but it's a thistle.

We should also avoid causing friendship fatigue. Proverbs says, "Let your foot be seldom in your neighbor's house, lest he have his fill of you and hate you" (25:17). This isn't saying that we shouldn't spend significant time with our friends. It is saying we shouldn't smother them.

2. How Not to Sharpen Your Friends

Proverbs also promotes gentleness by warning about strife. "Iron sharpens iron, and one man sharpens another" (Prov. 27:17). Many have understood this to mean that two people help each other become wiser—we knock off rough edges through thoughtful dialogue. That kind of mental sharpening is certainly good. But that's probably not what this particular verse means.

The sharpening here is not a good thing. This pictures relational strife, not character sculpting. As the footnote in the ESV says, the Hebrew of this verse reads more literally, "Iron sharpens iron, and one man sharpens the face of another." In Proverbs, when parts of a face sharpen, watch out. Sharp eyes glare like a dagger. A sharp tongue speaks words like sword thrusts. Facial features sharpen like weapons. And think about the image here: to sharpen iron, one piece of iron was put in the furnace to soften, then another iron hammer beat it until it became sharp. This is a negative image, and we find it in the context of a number of negative relationship images. In light of this, Ron Giese summarizes the verse this way: "Just as a hard iron hammer pounds soft iron into something sharp, ready for battle, in the same way a man causes his neighbor to go on the attack."[8] The implication? Don't provoke people to anger.

Do people put up their defenses around you? Perhaps it's because you speak offensively around them. Maybe you like to "speak your mind," make fun of friends, or you're easily agitated. If so, you may prepare people's faces for battle rather than friendship.

Proverbs 12:18 says that our "rash words are like sword thrusts." Rash words are thoughtless critiques, passive-aggressive responses, and sarcastic remarks. A pattern of sarcastic speech doesn't feel like sword thrusts to people, but more like incessant paper cuts. In some friendship groups, it functions as an expected form of friendly joking. Sarcasm used to be the way I expressed affection to people. But sometimes my remarks hit too close to home. And I wasn't sensitive enough to notice when someone felt ganged up on. I'm thankful for one person who let me know how I came across to some people. My sarcasm didn't fit the standard of "only such as is good for building up, as fits the occasion, that it may give grace to those who hear" (Eph. 4:29).

When we remember how God speaks to all who are in Christ—with sheer, undeserved kindness, encouraging us with the strength of his love and the hope of his promises—how then should we speak to one another? As we receive God's kind-hearted speech to us, we'll begin replacing friendly fire with something truly friendly.

3. Destroying Friendship with a Whisper

Finally, avoid gossip. Like a strong tower, a friendship can take years to build. And Proverbs says that it can collapse with words—with a mere whisper.

"A whisperer separates close friends," and "he who repeats a matter separates close friends" (Prov. 16:28; 17:9). The Hebrew word for "close friends" is *alluph*, the strongest word for friendship. Think of your closest relationships right now—it just takes a whisper to break them apart.

What kind of whisper? Spreading secrets. Gossip destroys friendship because it destroys trust, and trust is the foundation of friendship. If I can't trust a friend, I'm not going to open up anymore. I'm going to shut the door of transparency and turn the deadbolt. If I know that anything I tell someone may make its way to everyone else, I'm not going to share it. We see this kind of sacred trust embodied in Esther Burr's journal entry about her friend: "Mrs. Smith and I were talking . . . and determined that whatever had been spoken in confidence while there was supposed to be friendship ought to be kept a secret. Although the friendship was at an end, yet the obligation was strong as ever."[9]

The Soil of Self

All of these weeds find nourishment in the soil of self-focus. We speak and act inconsiderately when we don't pay attention to the emotions of others. We cause strife when we care more about self-expression than a peaceful relationship. We spread a bad report about someone because we care more about advancing our own reputation than damaging our friend's.

Our hearts default to a posture of self-focus. I instinctively place myself at the center of my relationships. I tend to think about how *others* have wronged *me*—how they have been inconsiderate, have expressed anger, or have gossiped about me. In truth, though, the roots of these weeds find fertile soil in my own soul as well.

If we mainly think about the weeds that others need to uproot, and not our own, our relationships won't flourish. Because this very impulse—this tendency to think about how *they* have failed *us*, rather than how *we* have failed *them*—is self-centered, and it will produce weeds. In order to cultivate true friendship, then, we must cultivate a posture of repentance.

And as we do this, we'll also give our friends grace. Because if we need our friends to be perfect friends, we will become terrible friends.

CONCLUSION

In the end, the best advice for cultivating friendship is not to *find* a better friend but to *become* one. And we do it by embracing this wisdom, putting in the work, and uprooting our weeds.

But we also need more than this. We need to know the deepest meaning and ultimate significance of friendship. What if every great friendship tapped into some greater reality of friendship? What if we found out that friendship is the meaning of the universe, and that God, as a great Friend, is restoring true friendship to the world? What if we could view all our feeble attempts at cultivating friendships as little echoes of a more glorious reality?

That would change everything.

QUESTIONS FOR REFLECTION AND DISCUSSION

1. If someone looked at how you spent your time last week (where you were, what you did, who you spent time with), what five

things would they conclude are most important to you? How highly do family and friendship rank?

2. What is one practical way that you will pursue more face-to-face time with friends? What is one rhythm that you want to establish in order to get more side-by-side time with friends?

3. From the suggestions about finding friendship around the table, what is one friendship rhythm you can plan to add to your life right now?

4. Who in your life has modeled oxygen-giving affirmation and encouragement? What are a few ways they encourage people that you want to imitate?

5. Which of the three relational weeds do you see as most prevalent in your own life? What is one way you can uproot it?

PART 3

THE REDEMPTION OF FRIENDSHIP

6

A BIBLICAL THEOLOGY
OF FRIENDSHIP

The entire history of redemption—in a sense—is a giant, cosmic act of friendship.

Timothy Keller

One of the most famous lines in English literature is the climactic sentence in Charles Dickens's novel *A Tale of Two Cities*: "It is a far, far better thing that I do, than I have ever done; it is a far, far better rest that I go to than I have ever known." These were Sydney Carton's last words. Another man, Charles Darnay, was expecting to be executed. But Sydney, out of love for his friend, managed to take his place. It is one of the only good things Sydney had ever done, and it is the noblest thing he ever could do. He gave his life for his friend.

Stories of courageous sacrifice like this one pervade Western literature and movies. Why do they resonate so deeply with us?

Because the stories that we love echo the story in which we live, the center of which blazes with the greatest act of friendship history has ever known: Jesus's sacrifice for his friends.

According to the Bible, history travels along a plotline. Its narrative arc develops through a series of covenants, and the theme of friendship appears with almost every one of them. Scripture tells a story of reconciliation, and the main character is God, who, at great cost to himself, turns his enemies into his dear friends. Thus, there is a biblical theology of friendship—that is, friendship is a whole-Bible theme, and it helps us understand the Bible's unfolding storyline and unified message.

And this cosmic story of friendship actually gives us the motivation we need to carry out the vision of the last three chapters. How we view God, and how we understand our place in the world, inevitably shapes how we live. As we learn to see ourselves in this story—the true story of the world—we find ourselves transformed to become better friends. What is the story?

In short: God walked with us in friendship. We walked away. And now he's befriending us again.

GOD'S SPREADING GOODNESS

What comes to mind when you think of eternity past, before the world began? Those endless ages were not empty; they surged with the holy love of the triune God. The Father, Son, and Spirit were eternally engaged in joyful communion. Jesus said, "Father, . . . you loved me before the foundation of the world" (John 17:24). He prayed this on the night before he died. He asked that his followers would be one, "even as we are one" and "just as you, Father, are in me, and I in you" (17:11, 21). This prayer presses human language to its limits as it shows the triune God's inner life of love. The Father, Son, and Spirit are one in essence and thus deeply united in fellowship. God is utterly unique as our Creator, so our fellowship is not exactly like his. Yet he made us in his image, so the friendship we experience reflects something of his own trinitarian life of love.

Some may view the Trinity as a theological difficulty. But the Trinity is not a math problem to be solved; it is a marvel to behold. Here's why: the Trinity shows us that ultimate reality is not eternal nothingness. It is not eternal matter. It is not an eternal force. Ultimate reality is personal, relational, and exuberantly joyful. Before there was anything, there was love. There was, in a sense, friendship.

Jesus's prayer also shows his deepest heart for his people. He wants them to know this relational joy, to enter into it, and to share in it. Jesus's great burden was (and is) that we might experience something of the love that is found in God himself: "That the love with which you have loved me may be in them, and I in them" (17:26; see 14:17, 21, 23). Why was this so strongly on his heart that night before he died? Because it was *always* on his heart. This is an everlasting desire. As Charles Spurgeon put it, "In the heart of our Lord Jesus there burns such friendship towards us that all other forms of it are as dim candles to the sun."[1]

This is, in fact, why creation exists. God is like a bubbling spring, a fountain overflowing with the refreshing waters of life. Like a rushing waterfall, the joy of God's triune fellowship overflowed, creating a world that would share in his love. God has a "spreading goodness."[2] One of the central reasons why God made us was to befriend us.

God didn't need to create anything. He was fully happy and satisfied in himself. Yet he did create. Not to fill a deficiency but to overflow from his fullness. Kevin Vanhoozer explains, "The

God of the Christian gospel is the Father, Son, and Spirit working in perfect communion for an even greater communion."[3]

This is why history is what it is: a story of friendship. What else would we expect, given the God who wrote it? Communal love marks God's very nature, which shows itself in true friendship. And so history begins, flowing from the heart of God.

WALKING WITH GOD IN PARADISE

God designed our world for true fellowship—with God and with one another. Adam was alone at first and, as we saw in chapter 2, that was "not good" (Gen. 2:18). He could not fully reflect God's relational love—not in isolation. Therefore, God created Eve so that both of them would enjoy the gift of friendship through marriage. And God commissioned them to multiply so that future generations would fill the world with society. Their marriage was not just the first friendship; it filled the world with friendships.

Eden was also the place of friendship with God. Adam and Eve did not just enjoy fellowship horizontally (with one another), but also vertically (with God). God made us to enjoy his presence. In Eden, heaven and earth were joined together. God dwelt with his people. And he walked with them in friendship.

According to Genesis 3:8, Adam and Eve "heard the sound of the LORD God walking in the garden in the cool of the day." This is most likely a relational image. The description of God "walking" in Eden is one of a number of parallels between Eden and Israel's later tabernacle and temple.[4] God instituted those future sanctuaries as symbolic reminders of his once-intimate relationship with humanity. They were each a mini-Eden, reverberating with echoes of this first paradise. And the center of these sanctuaries reflected the very heart of Eden: the presence of God. Echoing God's "walking" in Genesis 3:8, God later referred to his presence in the tabernacle, saying, "I will walk among you and will be your God" (Lev. 26:12).[5] Thus, Israel's later sanctuaries pointed backward to the ideal relationship of Eden, where God walked among his people.

This gives us a glimpse into the ideal relationship between God and humanity. In paradise, God walked with his people in friendship.

But it didn't last.

THE FIRST BROKEN FRIENDSHIPS

Proverbs warns against the "whisperer" who separates close friends (Prov. 16:28). Satan was the first one. He slipped into the garden to sever the first friendships, and he did it by subtly slandering God's friendly heart: If God were truly your friend, would he keep you from that tree? What is he hiding? Listen, friends, can you really trust him?

The whispers worked. Before Adam and Eve disobeyed God's law, they already doubted his love. Satan offered them a cup of distrust—which is always the poison of friendship—and they each drank it down. They ate the fruit because they already drank this cup. The essence of sin is not merely breaking rules; it is breaking trust. Every sin is rebellion against God's authority, but it is also a rejection of his friendship.

Under every sin lies a failure to trust God's heart.

Sin, because it is inherently antisocial, always ruins relationships. This story shows us three ways in which sin damages friendship. First, sin separates. Adam and Eve quickly covered themselves with leaves. As they hid, transparency and emotional safety fled. Second, affection cools. Adam quickly shifted the blame to Eve, then they both turned adversarial. Finally, friendships end. Sin produced death—first spiritual, then physical—and death now separates even the closest friends.

Sin also broke Adam and Eve's friendship with God. They hid when they heard his approach (Gen. 3:8). Adam even blamed *God* for giving Eve to him as a companion: "The woman *whom you gave to be with me*, she gave me fruit of the tree." (3:12). God originally answered Adam's isolation with this wife and friend. Yet Adam insinuated that this was where the problem began.

So God sent them out of Eden. Now every one of us enters the world oriented away from true friendship. But God will bring us back. Sin separated these friends, but the whisperer will not have the last word. God will. And so he clothed Adam and Eve with a promise—a token of his friendship: the whispering Serpent will be crushed by a Warrior Son (3:15).

THE BEFRIENDING GOD

From here, the Bible tells the story of reconciliation. One of our first glimpses of restored friendship appears in a quite unlikely place: a genealogy. The list of names in Genesis 5 repeats the phrase "and he died." Every death, in every generation, confirms that sin remained and friendships ended. Yet one man broke the pattern: Enoch, who didn't die but "walked with God, and he was not, for God took him" (v. 24). Genesis 5 singles out Enoch from the rest of humanity and summarizes this man's life with this one remarkable phrase: he "walked with God." Later, Noah also "walked with God" (6:9). Throughout the Old Testament, we read of people walking *before* God or walking *in* his commands; but only Enoch and Noah walked *with* God. This metaphor uniquely refers to the intimacy of friendship.[6]

This also reminds us of Eden. Enoch and Noah, like Adam and Eve before them, walked with God. And what did they find as a result of friendship with God? Enoch found unending life instead of death, and Noah found deliverance instead of destruction. Here, even on the first pages of the Bible, we find God as the great friend of sinners.

And he has a plan. God will reconcile people to himself from every generation and every nation. But God's plan to befriend many comes through his relationship with one. God called Abraham "my friend" (Isa. 41:8; also 2 Chron. 20:7). James later wrote that Abraham "was called a friend of God" (James 2:23).

In Genesis 18, God treated Abraham as a friend when he was about to destroy Sodom and Gomorrah. He didn't need to tell Abraham these plans. Yet he said, "Shall I hide from Abraham what I am about to do?" (Gen. 18:17). He added, "For I have known him"—a deeply relational idea (v. 19 ESV alternate reading). Thomas Goodwin observed here that God "could not do a great thing, but he must tell his friend of it. He speaks as one shackled and restrained by the laws of friendship."[7] Abraham then interceded for Sodom, and he did so quite boldly, as only a friend would dare. This conversation was full of transparency and candor.

There in Genesis 18, God treated *Abraham* as a friend, but then in Genesis 22, Abraham treats *God* as a friend. God tested him by asking him to sacrifice his son, and Abraham showed unwavering faith. He trusted that God could even raise his son from the dead. This is why James called Abraham God's friend (James 2:21–23). His loyalty proved his friendship—this is James's point. Abraham's obedience *to* God demonstrated his faith *in* God, which proved his friendship *with* God.

God chose Abraham to be the one through whom he would restore Eden's lost blessings (Gen. 12:1–3). Through Abraham, God will restore true friendship for us—vertical friendship (with

God) and horizontal friendships (with one another). God's mission is to create a community of friends who know him as the greatest Friend.

Centuries later we meet another friend of God. Abraham's line multiplied, they became the people of Israel, and they suffered under Egyptian oppression. So God appointed Moses to deliver them. In the tent of meeting, outside Israel's camp, Moses regularly met with God. There, "the LORD used to speak to Moses face to face, as a man speaks to his friend" (Ex. 33:11). God brought Moses close, not just to speak as a king to his servant but as one friend to another. They talked together as friends. This intimacy would later become one of the primary ways in which Israel remembered Moses: He was the one "whom the LORD knew face to face" (Deut. 34:10). He was one who knew God as a Friend.

BROKEN FRIENDSHIPS AND A BETTER PROMISE

To this point, we've seen Scripture describe Enoch, Noah, Abraham, and Moses as friends of God. They knew God personally and intimately. Yet Israel as a whole didn't experience this. They didn't recover the lost fellowship of Eden. The rest of the Old Testament story shows this in several ways.

First, God's people, as a whole, remained distant from him. God delivered Israel in order to dwell with them, but he kept them at a distance. God invited Moses to climb Mount Sinai, but the people trembled at its base (Ex. 19:16–20). God walked in the tabernacle as he did in Eden, but the people could not enter (Lev. 26:12). God invited Moses to speak as a friend, but Israel only watched (Ex. 33:7–11). God knew Moses face to face, but even later prophets did not experience this level of intimacy again (Deut. 34:10).

Second, God's people did not prove to be his faithful friends. They rebelled from the beginning. They distrusted God, and this led to disordered loves and disobedient lives. God offered them friendship, but they rejected it.

Third, they were also unfaithful to each other. Some enjoyed true friendship: Ruth and Naomi, and David and Jonathan, for instance. But Israel's relationships disintegrated and society declined. As Israel moved toward exile, Jeremiah told them they could no longer trust even a brother or a friend (Jer. 9:4–5). Malachi rebuked each man for breaking covenant with his wife, whom he called "your companion"—your dear friend (Mal. 2:14). Micah said, "Put no trust in a neighbor; have no confidence in a friend" (Mic. 7:5). Here's what this shows us: as Israel rejected God's offer of divine friendship, they lost the capacity to enjoy human friendship. So Israel went into exile just like Adam and Eve before; God sent them away from his presence (Jer. 52:3).

Yet the story still moves toward restoration. God's covenants with his people carry the Bible's storyline forward. Each major covenant successively builds on the others, moving toward the restoration of the friendship we lost in Eden.

God made the first four major covenants in this story with Adam, Noah, Abraham, and Moses, and the theme of divine friendship appeared with each of them. In fact, apart from its connection to Enoch (who was unique in that he never died), friendship with God *only* explicitly appeared at these covenantal high points of the story. The people whom the Old Testament most clearly identified as God's friends—Adam, Noah, Abraham, and Moses—were the mediators of Scripture's first four major covenants.[8]

Scripture points its finger to these covenant mediators as friends of God. But it does not do this for everyone within these covenants. Those whom the Old Testament explicitly highlights as God's friends are not all the people *within* the covenants, but especially the mediators *of* the covenants. Of course, other men and women who truly trusted God throughout the Old Testament knew something of his friendship—they knew his affection, his counsel, and so forth.[9] Yet Scripture primarily defines their relationship with God in terms of *servanthood*; God is the Lord, and Israel is his servant.

So several questions arise: Will God make a covenant in which he gives friendship to *everyone* within it? Could God make a covenant that restores the level of friendship that we lost in Eden? Might this covenant not only restore divine friendship but also bring us into flourishing relationships with each other? The prophets did not understand all that God intended when he promised a new covenant, but he was answering these questions.

NO LONGER CALLED SERVANTS

After several centuries, the friend of sinners arrived. Jesus came to befriend sinners and bring them into a new covenant.

On the night before his crucifixion, Jesus presided over the meal that inaugurated this covenant. Jesus announced that a great transition was taking place. The hinge of redemptive history was turning, and the way God related to his people was changing. Jesus announced to his disciples: "No longer do I call you servants . . . I have called you friends" (John 15:15). This "no longer . . . but now" moment "signals a new era in salvation history."[10]

In the old covenant, God honored his people by calling them his servants. We still have this privilege today. But we are now also *more* than servants; we are his friends. And Jesus gives his friendship to all who trust him. Unlike the old covenant, every member in the new covenant enjoys personal friendship with God. Jesus came to finally and forever recover friendship. As Jonathan Edwards wrote, "There is a covenant of mutual friendship and love that Christ offers to all that will accept of his friendship."[11]

How does Jesus secure this relationship? Through his death and resurrection. When he called his disciples his friends, he also said, "Greater love has no one than this, that someone lay down his life for his friends" (John 15:13). Jesus wanted them to grasp the meaning of what he was about to do for them. He wanted them to understand the very purpose for which he came. He wanted them to discern the deep things of the gospel: that the cross is a cosmic act of friendship. He came to die, and to die for his friends.

THE FRIENDLY RADIANCE OF GOD'S GLORY

God's glory is a major theme in the Gospel of John. John shows us that God reveals his glory most clearly in Jesus's life and, surprisingly, also in his death (John 17:1).

How does God reveal his glory through the life of Christ? Through love and, according to John, specifically *through the love of friendship*. New Testament scholar Richard Bauckham notes that Jesus's love for his friends "is probably the most theologically important way in which [John's] Gospel depicts Jesus as God incarnate in humanity."[12] He writes, "It is in this thoroughly human love of Jesus for his friends that the divine love for the world takes human form."[13] The radiant glory of God's love takes human expression in Jesus's love for his friends.

John also shows us that God reveals his glory most clearly (and counterintuitively) through Jesus's death. The Romans reserved the spectacle of crucifixion for their worst criminals. But John says that Jesus's crucifixion displayed *glory*. How? As the greatest conceivable act of love. Nothing reveals God's glory more than the dying love of Christ. That is *the* place where his glory shone most radiantly in all of world history. John shows us that we will not behold its full luster unless we understand it as an act of friendship. God displays his glory through Christ's love, and Jesus says there is no greater love than laying down one's life for friends (John 15:13).

Some people think of God's glory mainly as his greatness. They think of God's glory in terms of his power, his vastness. They think of God's glory reflected in the sunsets and stars. That's right, but when John shows us the blazing center of God's glory, he doesn't point to the sky. He points to the cross, where the Son of God laid his life down for his friends. This is love. This is beauty. This is his greatest glory.

If you want to know God's glory, look at Christ's love. And if you want to look at Christ's love, look at the cross, where he died for his friends. Jesus's sacrifice—for you and me, if we'll have him—is the resplendent radiance of God's glory.

How, then, do we see the greatness of God's heart? We see it in the great length he goes to befriend us.

HE SAVES US TO BEFRIEND US

The cross is a heroic act of friendship because it is the greatest act of sacrifice. Jesus received the opposite of what he deserved to save us from exactly what we deserve. And what is that? The hellish experience of abject loneliness. He cried out, "My God, my God, why have you forsaken me?" (Matt. 27:46; Mark 15:34). Jesus is the only one who didn't deserve this cosmic isolation. Yet he took our hell and judgment so that we could receive his hand in friendship. Jesus was locked out so we could be let in.

Jesus was profoundly separated so that we could be permanently befriended.

Here's how the apostle Paul put it: "In Christ God was reconciling the world to himself, not counting their trespasses against them" (2 Cor. 5:19). This verse brings three key ideas together. First, *reconciliation*, which means, "to restore a relationship, to renew a friendship."[14] God created the world in friendship, but we became his enemies. God could have disregarded us and started over, but he didn't—because his love is too great for that. Second, *justification*. God restores friendship by not counting our sins against us. He forgives us and declares us righteous. Third, *substitution*. God accepts us as righteous because Jesus died on the cross, in our place, for our sins. He took the punishment we deserve so that we could get the blessing only he deserves. "For our sake he made him to be sin who knew no sin, so that in him we might become the righteousness of God" (5:21). This is the great cost of our salvation. The cross shows us how bad we are (we deserve *that*!), but it also shows us just how much God loves us. This is the truth at the center of the universe: God wanted us to become his friends more than he wanted his Son to avoid hell.

The central message of the New Testament is *reconciliation through justification because of substitution*. God made us his friends (reconciliation) by not counting our sins against us (justification) because Jesus died for us (substitution).

God saves us to befriend us.

Christians love the truth of our justification in Christ. But we treasure this because it brings us to God. And it's not that God has justified us, so now he's stuck with us—our friendship is *his* idea. He decisively justifies us because he decidedly wants us. As Puritan Walter Marshall put it, "Justification is God's way of taking you into friendship with himself."[15]

THE NEW COMMUNITY OF FRIENDS

The cross is also God's way of bringing us into deep friendship with others. Eden was originally the place of divine *and* human friendship. And the treacherous sin in Eden didn't just result in broken friendship with God; it also unleashed the dynamics that make friendship so challenging in our own lives. But now, as we find ourselves reconciled to God, we also receive our welcome into a new community.

Jesus taught us to live and love as a community of friends. He gave us a new-covenant "new commandment" (John 13:34). He said, "This is my commandment, that you love one another as I have loved you" (15:12). At first glance, this doesn't sound very new—the Old Testament commanded Israel to love their neighbors, as themselves. So what is actually *new* here? This: the standard is ratcheted up and defined in terms of friendship. We must now love one another *as Jesus loved us*. And how did he love us? He clarifies this with his very next statement: "Greater love has no one than this, that someone lay down his life for his friends" (v. 13). Jesus makes the great love command even greater—by clothing it with sacrificial friendship. We are not just to "love our neighbor as ourselves"; we are to love one another sacrificially *as friends*. We are to love one another with the same kind of befriending love that Jesus showed us at the cross.

The newness of the new commandment is all about friendship. Jesus loved us as friends; now we love his friends as our own.

The New Testament repeatedly portrays the church as a community of friends. For example, Acts 4:32 says, "The full number of those who believed were of one heart and soul, and no one said that any of the things that belonged to him was his own, but they had everything in common." This reflects the Roman ideals of friendship in which two people share "one soul" and "have all things in common."[16] What the Romans held out as an ideal, the early church practiced as normal, even across ethnic and socio-economic divides.

Where did Peter and John go after being released from prison? "They went to their friends" (4:23). John later referred to a local church as, simply, "the friends" (3 John 15). He longed to see them "face to face," as one friend speaks to another (2 John 12; 3 John 14). He wanted them to "have fellowship with us; and indeed our fellowship is with the Father and with his Son Jesus Christ" (1 John 1:3).

New Testament scholar Gordon Fee has called Paul's letter to the Philippians a letter of friendship.[17] He notes, "Friendship in particular is radically transformed from a two-way to a three-way bond—between [Paul], the Philippians, and Christ."[18] So it is with all Christian friendship.

While a local church is a community of friends, each one of us will still only experience the marks of true friendship with a few people. The "one anothers" of the New Testament—forgive one another, bear one another's burdens, and so forth—these are marks of friendship, and we only fulfill them in close relationships. Each local church is a true "community of friends" when it is filled with many smaller, overlapping networks of deep friendships.

According to the New Testament, true friendship is not optional. Hebrews 3:13–14 urges Christians to "exhort one another every day . . . that none of you may be hardened by the deceitfulness of sin. For we have come to share in Christ, if indeed we hold our original confidence firm to the end." We will only be saved in the end if we hold fast to Christ, and this requires friendship. This assumes Christians know each other deeply, contact one another frequently, and speak to one another frankly. Perseverance in the faith is the fruit of friendship.

The church is also a befriending community, inviting others into friendship with Jesus and his people. Christians are not only reconciled to God; they are also entrusted with the ministry of reconciliation (2 Cor. 5:18–20). In other words, the church, as a community of Jesus's friends, welcomes others into this great friendship.

The missional church is a befriending church.

FRIENDSHIP FOREVER

Jesus said there will be no marriage in the new creation (Matt. 22:30). In this sense, we will all end up single. But single does not mean solitary. Christian marriages will give way to the greater marriage between Christ and the church, but the best part of every marriage will remain, which is friendship.

This means that for all who know Christ, whether single or married, the joys of friendship begin in this age and will never end. Apart from Christ, every relationship will end. But in Christ, every friendship only gets better and continues forever.

Scripture concludes with a symbolic vision of the new creation. The final chapters of Revelation highlight two aspects of our future. First, the new creation will be a happy world of human friendship. Revelation describes it as a city, filled with God's people. Friendship is not a temporary luxury for this age alone; it is also a permanent fixture of our eternal home. In other words, it never was, nor will it ever be, good for us to be alone.

Second, God will be our great Friend. Revelation describes the city as a perfect cube, which is a symbolic reminder of the other cube in Scripture: the temple's Most Holy Place, which symbolized God's presence back in Eden. God's presence will fill every corner of the new creation. Revelation 22 portrays the new creation as a new and better Eden where we will walk in friendship with God again.

All of God's people will "see his face, and his name will be on their foreheads" (Rev. 22:4). Moses spoke with God "face to face," but he never actually saw God (Ex. 33:20). Israel's high priest had God's name written on his forehead, allowing him alone to enter the Most Holy Place. These were each symbols, pointing backward to the lost fellowship in Eden and looking forward to the restored fellowship to come. In the new creation *every* believer will enter God's presence and see his face.

Many people think that eternal life will be boring. But think about your most joyful moments with friends. Now take that joy, multiply it by ten thousand, and project it into your eternal future. The whole of that happiness merely gestures in the direction of the joys to come. History ends with neither a bang nor a whimper, but with the laughter of friends.

History tells the drama of friendship created, lost, and then restored.

God loves his people with an everlasting and befriending love. He has loved us from eternity past and every moment of our lives. And so it will be forever, for all who trust him. God is our everlasting Friend, and our future is a world of friendship.

What if we could know this great Friend, personally, even now—this very moment?

QUESTIONS FOR REFLECTION AND DISCUSSION

1. What is your favorite example of self-sacrifice from literature, a movie, or life experience? Why do you think these kinds of stories affect us so strongly?

2. What is the most sacrificial thing a friend has ever done for you? What is the most sacrificial thing you have done for a friend?

3. What are two things Christians can do to experience true friendship in the context of the local church? What is one next step you will take to model this in your own life?

4. Our eternal home is a world of friendship, and it's only for those who are reconciled to God in this life. How should this motivate Christians to share the gospel—the good news of reconciliation through justification because of substitution—with others?

7

THE GREAT FRIEND

God's friendship is more precious than that of the
whole world.
Martin Luther

As you've read to this point in the book, maybe you've become
convinced that true friendship is hard to find. Perhaps you wonder if you'll ever find it, or find it again. Or maybe you're uncer-
tain if you will be able to give friendship the time, transparency,
and commitment it requires. Maybe you're discouraged because
you realize you have often failed to be a true friend—you've broken a friendship, you've distanced yourself from people, you've
made a mess of relationships. The more I consider the nature of
true friendship, the more I see my own feeble attempts at friendship for what they are.

But what if you could have a friend who knew you better
than anyone, better than you even know yourself? And what
if, knowing everything, he still loved you, and even liked you?

And what if you could have a friend who, by his very relationship with you, would transform you to become a better friend to others?

You can. His name is Jesus. He's called the friend of sinners.

SHOULD WE—DARE WE, EVEN—CALL HIM FRIEND?

The idea of friendship with Jesus may sit uneasily with you. It sounds to some people like Christianity-lite—frothy, sentimental, maybe even irreverent. If you dismiss the notion of friendship with Jesus because you think it means superficial chumminess, I understand. But that's not what Jesus means. When he calls us friends, he means true friendship—the kind that we've been thinking about in this book.

But even if we acknowledge that real friendship isn't sentimental, friendship with Jesus may still seem unfitting to you. If Jesus is holy—the divine King who calms storms with a word, who upholds the universe by the word of his power, who receives glory and honor and praise—then doesn't it demean him to treat him as a friend? Does this not make Jesus seem less glorious, less lordly?

Just the opposite is true: friendship with Jesus is pure grace, and grace is the apex of his glory.

When we see Jesus as the Holy One, radiant in splendor, we behold glory. But when this same exalted King offers himself to us in friendship, we don't see less glory; we see *more*. Because we behold not just regal power but riches of grace (Eph. 1:7). Christ's glory shone in the humility of his incarnation and his cross, where he became one of us and died for us. And he died not just to pardon us as enemies—allowing us into his kingdom, but nudging us into the corner—but to welcome us as dear friends.

This sounds even more surprising when we consider just how holy *he* is and just how sinful *we* are. The Pharisees watched with narrowed eyes as Jesus sought out even the worst of sinners for friendship. They didn't think that sharing meals with sinners befit a holy messiah. So, when they called him a friend of sinners, they meant it as an insult (Luke 7:34). They didn't know that this actually demonstrated his true greatness. I wonder if any name gave him more pleasure, "for it expressed with perfect accuracy the true end and aim of His life."[1] According to the Pharisees, befriending sinners was a great expression of evil. According to Jesus, it was the highest expression of love.

Yet you still may wonder: How can we enjoy Jesus as our Friend if we're also called to obey him as our King? Some people view these two roles as incompatible. But kingship and companionship don't conflict. When Jesus calls us his friends, he still requires us to obey him: "You are my friends if you do what I command you," he said (John 15:14). Why does he tell his friends to obey him? Because even though he calls us friends, he remains the King. He is not a king *or* a companion; he is both. He tells *us* to obey *him*; we never tell *him* to obey *us*.

When we see Jesus as both of these at the same time—not awkwardly alternating between them at different moments but trusting Jesus as both exalted King *and* intimate Friend—it kindles worship in our hearts. If we only consider Jesus as one of these, it's like trying to keep the fire of our hearts lit with only one isolated log. But when we bring both of these together, placing one flaming log on another, the fire burns hotter and brighter. Charles Spurgeon brings them together, and you can sense the light and heat it produced in his soul:

> It is a mark of wonderful condescension on His part that He should call us His friends and it confers upon us the highest

conceivable honor that such a Lord as He is, so infinitely superior to us, should condescend to enter into terms of friendship with us. . . . That I should be Your friend—nothing but Your loving, condescending tenderness could ever have conceived of this![2]

This is what happens when we draw near to the real Jesus, who is both our worthy Lord and beloved Friend.

THE FRIEND OF SINNERS

No one is born into fellowship with Jesus. We have all acted like faithless—worse than faithless, *treacherous*—friends. James says, "Whoever wishes to be a friend of the world makes himself an enemy of God" (James 4:4). We each lean away from, not toward, God's friendship. Yet the Father sent his Son to welcome sinners. He sent him not to condemn but to befriend anyone who will have him (John 3:17). And when we open ourselves up to him with trust, he ties us to himself in an irrevocable bond, a covenant of friendship.

What does this mean? Jesus is the truest, the best, the ultimate Friend. Here are five glimpses of the surpassing greatness of the greatest Friend.

He Loves Us with the Deepest Affection

Jesus befriends us with affection. He makes us his friends, and he has no reservations whatsoever. And he never will. If you are his friend, then he has set his heart on you, and it will never be moved. He loves you with an everlasting love (Jer. 31:3). He loves you with all his heart, and he always will.

That Jesus is our Friend means that he doesn't just love us but that he's *glad* to love us. We do not enter into a mere contract or partnership or a vaguely defined relationship with him. We enter into real friendship, with all of the affection and enjoyment that comes with it. Friends enjoy each other. They *like* each other.

They also miss and long to see each other. Think about the future return of Christ. Do you look forward to seeing him? Not as much as he looks forward to seeing you. He left to prepare a place for us, and he asked his Father that we would live with him forever (John 14:3; 17:24; 2 Tim. 4:18). He sits on the edge of his throne, so to speak, waiting for the Father's word. And when he returns, he will judge the world. Does that frighten you? Consider this: If he is your Friend now, then he will not cease to be your Friend in that great moment of judgment. He will gladly count all your sins as forgiven, and he will even find things to affirm and commend in you (Matt. 25:21; 1 Cor. 4:5; 1 Pet. 1:7).

One of the most pressing questions of our lives, often buried deep in the subconscious, is this: What does God think of me? In all my failings, in all my weakness—how does he *feel* about me? If you trust Christ, you can answer that question: He loves you as his dear friend.

But what about when we've sinned against him? What then? Yes, he is rightly disappointed. But how does someone feel when a son or daughter or dear friend makes a sinful mess of their life? Grieved, yes. But also stirred with compassion. A true friend draws near in times of need, even when the suffering is self-inflicted. God says to his rebellious people in Isaiah 43:4, "You are precious in my eyes, and honored, and I love you." Though we have forfeited any claim to his esteem, he gives it to us anyway. And he's happy to do it. He loves us from his deepest heart.

He Loves Us to the Very End

Jesus's love is constant and covenantal. He counts you as his friend, and he always will. We know this for three reasons.

First, Jesus will love us to the end because he already did—he loved us to death. On the night before he died, he took his disciples into an upper room to share a meal with them. Here's how the apostle John introduced that evening: "Having loved his own, . . . he loved them to the end" (John 13:1). The "end" refers to the cross, where Jesus bore the weight of our sins and the judgment of hell. And when he did it, he thought of "his own"—you and me, every one of us by name—and he thought of us as his dear friends: "Greater love has no one than this, that someone lay down his life for his friends" (15:13). Now, if he would do *that* for us, will he ever leave us? If he held fast to us in friendship then, will he ever let go?

You may think that you don't qualify for this, but on the very night when Jesus called the disciples friends, he knew they would soon desert him. He told them as much in that very conversation (13:37–38; 16:32). It was on the very night when he knew they would prove fickle that he decided to call them friends. And in the very moments when they deserted him, what did he do? He suffered for them—in a cosmic act of friendship. He befriends us knowing that we don't deserve a moment of it.

You may sometimes fail and forget him. But he will never fail or forget you.

Second, we know Jesus will love us to the end because he has already proven his constancy. You may have been abandoned by companions. The apostle Paul was. He said, "At my first defense no one came to stand by me, but all deserted me" (2 Tim. 4:16). In one of the most difficult moments of his life, when Paul needed his friends the most, they all abandoned him. "But," he said, "the Lord stood by me and strengthened me" (4:17). Paul used friendship language there. He needed someone to stay and strengthen him, so Jesus stepped in when everyone else stepped out. He does that for all who trust him. Charles Spurgeon wrote, "Christ is 'a friend that sticks closer than a brother.' . . . You have often left him; has he ever left you? You have had many trials and troubles; has he ever deserted you? Has he ever turned away his heart, and shut up his compassion? No, children of God, it is your solemn duty to say 'No,' and bear witness to his faithfulness."[3]

Third, he will love us to the end because he loved us before the beginning. "I have called you friends. . . . You did not choose me, but I chose you" (John 15:15–16). Friendship, by definition, requires choice. Jesus chose his friends, and he did it from eternity past. If the doctrine of election seems stale or cold to you, notice how Jesus clothes it in the warmth of friendship.

These are deep waters, and Thomas Goodwin helps us peer into them: "God has been your ancient friend, even from everlasting. . . . He has loved you ever since he loved himself. . . . There is not a moment in which he has not loved us, and had his thoughts upon us."[4]

If you are Jesus's friend, how do you know that he will always love you?

Because he always has.

A significant part of the Christian life is simply getting used to the fact that God actually loves us, freely and from his heart. And he always has, from eternity past.

He Lets Us All the Way In

Jesus is a transparent Friend. He opens his heart and shares his plans. He called the disciples his friends with this explanation: "For all that I have heard from my Father I have made known to you" (John 15:15). Friends speak with unguarded openness, and that's what Jesus gives us.

145

Jesus demonstrated this as he said it. John 13–17 records his conversation with his disciples on this final evening before he died. Through that conversation, he didn't just talk about friendship; he demonstrated it. He opened the window to his soul, and he shared his secrets. And he preserved it for us to read even today.

On that night, he explained his plans to sacrifice his life for us; to go to prepare a place for us; to send the Spirit to comfort and help us; to answer our prayers and fill us with joy; to return again to bring us to himself; to give us peace and turn our sorrows to joy. And then he prayed for us, for all his friends through all generations: "I do not ask for these only, but also for those who will believe in me through their word" (17:20).

These promises and prayers that Jesus shared with his first disciples remain his promises and prayers for all disciples. As we read the words he spoke to those friends *then*, we read the words he still speaks to his friends *today*. The Bible reveals Jesus's heart and his plans. It is, among other things, a letter of friendship.

He Stirs with Compassion

Jesus is an empathetic Friend. You may think he feels distant. You may think, *He is exalted up there; how could he care about me down here?*

But think back to Jesus's earthly ministry. When he stood at the tomb of his friend, Lazarus, he cried (John 11:35). Why? Because his friend died. And because he felt the distress of Lazarus's sisters, whom he also loved as friends.[5] Jesus wept with them. He felt what they felt. And if Jesus wept with them in their great sorrow, will he not weep with us in ours?

He did not only feel empathy in those few years of his earthy ministry. He continues to feel it this very moment. Those occasions we read about in Scripture don't just show us who he was for a limited time, but who he is forever. God the Son became incarnate in order to experience our human weakness and the full range of human emotions. He became human so that he could serve as our sympathetic High Priest, so that he could be our empathetic great Friend. If you are his disciple, he doesn't just know *what* you feel, he knows *how* it feels. And he feels it with you even now.

Maybe you sit sad and lonely, under ominous clouds in this season of life. Jesus knows. And he knows how it feels, because he has felt it before (Mark 14:32–36). He is, in this very moment, interceding for you (Heb. 7:25). Christ sympathizes with us with all his heart. And he is also able to help us with all his might. Christ is both willing and able to help us in our deepest needs.

If you are his, then you are his friend. He never has, and he never will, shut his heart to you.

He Speaks with Candor and Kindness

Jesus is a Friend who speaks with straightforward honesty. He speaks to us from his heart and for our good, always. This includes speech that may not at first sound friendly. Proverbs says that a true friend loves us enough to give us "faithful wounds" (Prov. 27:5–6). As a true friend, Jesus tells us what we need to hear even if it isn't always what we want to hear. He speaks the truth in love, delivering hard but necessary words.

This is, in fact, how our friendship with Jesus begins. The gospel is a message that stings before it makes us sing. The gospel wounds us in order to heal us. Jesus tells us that we are far more sinful than we had ever thought, and yet at the same time, he loves us so much that he died to make us his friends. When the gospel was first proclaimed after Jesus's resurrection, those who heard "were cut to the heart" (Acts 2:37). Jesus gave them "a heart wound" of conviction.[6] This is how the Christian life begins. And then as we follow Christ, he continues to deliver these faithful wounds as a faithful Friend.

Christ's affection, constancy, transparency, empathy, and candor show us the greatness of this great Friend. Jonathan Edwards wrote, "Whatsoever there is, or can be, that is desirable to be in a friend, is in Christ, and that to the highest degree that can be desired."[7] No one could possibly imagine a greater Friend than Jesus.

CULTIVATING FRIENDSHIP WITH CHRIST

If friendship is an affectionate bond forged between two people as they journey through life with openness and trust, what does this look like with Christ? How do we cultivate companionship with him moment by moment? We relate to Jesus as our *Prophet* by hearing his word. We relate to him as our *Priest* by receiving his sacrifice. We relate to him as our *King* by submitting to his authority. But how do we uniquely relate to him as our *Friend*? Here are six key ways to cultivate friendship with Christ.

1. The Privilege of Friendship

First, we receive the privilege of this relationship. When Jesus called his disciples friends, he contrasted it with the relationship of a servant to a master. In light of this, we should ask ourselves: Do we think of our relationship with him only in terms of servanthood or also in terms of friendship?

Consider these differences between a servant and a friend: The servant is only told what to do, but the friend is also told why. The servant merely obeys because he's told to, but the friend obeys because he wants to. The servant does things out of obligation, but the friend out of joy. The servant only comes when summoned, but the friend is welcome anytime. The servant brings food to the master, but the friend eats it with him. The servant only feels obligation in the relationship, but the friend feels privilege.

Do you enjoy the honor of this kind of relationship with Jesus yet? If you think you're not worthy of it, good. That means you understand. This is supposed to shock us, because we *don't* deserve it. The King of creation seeks out lowly rebels, not just to extend pardon but to welcome them into the closest companionship. Any humbled rebel would feel surprised and unworthy in the moment of this King's approach.

But don't refuse him because you feel unworthy. And don't work to earn his favor, either; that violates the very nature of friendship. Just receive it—on terms of grace, because of the cross—and happily offer to him all the grateful worship your heart can muster.

J. I. Packer wrote in his classic book *Knowing God* that we have "great incentive to worship and love God in the thought that, for some unfathomable reason, he wants me as his friend, and desires to be my friend, and has given his Son to die for me in order to realize this purpose."[8]

2. Union for Communion

Second, we enjoy communion with God. Jesus said to the church of Laodicea, "Behold, I stand at the door and knock. If anyone hears my voice and opens the door, I will come in to him and eat with him, and he with me" (Rev. 3:20). Many have thought that Jesus here offers salvation to those who don't yet have it. But Jesus directs these words to a church; he speaks to professing believers. And what does he offer? A meal. The first-century readers would know what this means: Jesus offers intimate fellowship, and he extends it to each of us today.

This is the great goal of our union with Christ. The Spirit pulls us into Christ by faith, that we might enjoy fellowship with the triune God. This is why God pursues us: that he might bring us to himself—to know him, to enjoy him, to commune with him forever. Our union is for communion.

Friendship is the goal of salvation and the ultimate end of our existence.

What does it look like, practically, to experience this? How do we enter into the personal reality of knowing Christ? One way is through the Lord's Supper, when the church gathers for bread and wine to remember our Redeemer. We rightly call this communion. Local churches eat the Lord's Supper as an expression of friendship with Christ and also with one another.

Most often, we enjoy friendship with God through conversation. Friends talk to one another. In our friendship with God, he speaks to us through Scripture, and we speak to him in prayer. Jonathan Edwards wrote, "By conversation, not only is friendship maintained and nourished, but the felicity [contented joy] of friendship is tasted and enjoyed. . . . Conversation between God and mankind in this world, is maintained by God's *word* on his part, and by *prayer* on ours."[9] God shares his heart with us through the Bible, and we share ours through prayer.

This means that we approach Scripture not just to learn information but to hear God's voice. Through it, he speaks to us as friends. He opens his heart to us.

And prayer is our personal response to him. Perhaps your prayer life sometimes looks more like calling 911—only in emergencies, quick with the details, and no sense of a personal relationship. But God invites us to treat him more like our closest companions—to talk often, to enjoy his presence, and to drop in just to thank him throughout the day.

Prayer is also an opportunity for us to gain perspective in his presence. When we have a patient listener, it provides space for us to articulate our thoughts and gain clarity about our lives. Prayer is the space for thinking about God's Word in his presence, and it is space to articulate our appropriate response to it. As we express our own hopes and desires to this patient Friend in response to his Word, we gain clarity about our own lives.

Time spent in the Bible and prayer is a central means of communing with God. As we immerse ourselves in Scripture, we hear God address us personally. And we pray not only to make requests but also to commune with him.

We do not use Bible reading and prayer as tools to get God to bless us. We use them to enjoy the fellowship we already have with him.

3. Covenantal Faithfulness

Third, we demonstrate our friendship through unwavering obedience. Friendship is not just a privilege to enjoy but also a responsibility to fulfill. If we claim to be friends *of* Jesus, we have to be friends *to* Jesus. Our posture toward him should look like Jonathan's toward David, who was his king and his friend: "Whatever you say, I will do for you" (1 Sam. 20:4). That is covenantal friendship.

This is what Jesus meant when he said, "You are my friends, if you do what I command you" (John 15:14). *If?* That may at first sound like a condition we must meet in order to become Jesus's friends. Is our obedience a prerequisite to entering into fellowship with Jesus? Thankfully, no. First, Jesus didn't say that we *become* his friends if we obey him, but that we already are. Even as he says this, he already considers his disciples his friends (15:15; see also v. 3), and he will soon lay his life down for them (15:13). And the very reason why he must lay his life down for them is due to their *dis*obedience. So, Jesus is not telling his disciples how they can become his friends; he is telling them how they must demonstrate the reality of their friendship with him. Our obedience doesn't earn this relationship with Jesus; it confirms it. Obedience *to* Jesus demonstrates the reality of friendship *with* Jesus.

Second, true friendship always entails responsibility. Jesus said that if we are his friends, then we will show it. We will respond to his affection with affection, to his transparency with transparency, to his faithfulness with faithfulness. Friendship always answers to friendship.

The apostle James makes this point with the example of Abraham. First, he proves Abraham's friendship with God by showing that Abraham trusted God with an authentic and active faith, a faith that he demonstrated through his obedience. Abraham's great act of obedience, his willingness to offer his beloved son to God, showed that he truly believed, and therefore "'it was counted to him as righteousness'—*and he was called a friend of God*" (James 2:23). In other words, Abraham was called a friend *of* God because he demonstrated friendship *to* God. Second, James holds Abraham up as a pattern for every Christian. All who possess the active faith of Abraham are not only counted righteous but are also called friends.

God has shown his faithfulness to us, so how should we respond in return? Jesus gave his life for us; now we give ours to him.

Jesus's cosmic act of friendship at the cross transforms our whole outlook on disobedience. It changes our very emotional disposition toward sin. Because when we see the cross as an act of friendship, we also see what caused it—our own treacherous sin against him. "If Christ has died for me," Spurgeon said, "I cannot trifle with the evil that killed my best Friend."[10] If our sins caused our great Friend such agony, how can we enjoy them anymore? And if we know that our best Friend is now in heaven, with his great heart of love grieved by every one of our sins, we cannot treat disobedience flippantly. We may never get caught, but our best Friend knows. He died for that sin. And his heart grieves even now.

The more we know Jesus as our Friend, the more emotionally disagreeable it becomes to sin against him. Or, to look at this from a different angle: If we find it easy to sin against Jesus, then it's because we've tuned out his faithful wounds of rebuke. In other words, the more easily we are able to sin against Jesus, the less we truly know him as our Friend.

4. Never Alone, Never Unknown

Fourth, Jesus's friendship means that we are never truly alone, and we are never fully unknown. No matter how lonely you feel, you belong—that's what it means to know Jesus as a Friend. You may feel like an outsider to everyone everywhere, but if you belong to Jesus, then you *belong*. He made you his own (John 13:1; Phil. 3:12). Everyone else may forsake you, but one will always remain. As J. C. Ryle said, "No one need ever say I have no 'friend' to turn to, so long as Christ is in heaven."[11]

John Paton, a Scottish missionary in the South Pacific islands in the 1800s, knew what it meant to be, as he put it, "alone, all alone," and with his life at risk. With gunshots all around, he climbed a tree for safety. In his autobiography, he describes the event as it unfolded around him, and then he turns to us, the readers, and asks this question: "If thus thrown back upon your own soul, alone, all alone, in the midnight, in the bush, in the very embrace of death itself, have you a Friend that will not fail you then?"[12] Paton did, and he asks each one of us to consider if we do too.

Jesus's companionship means that we are never truly unknown. Maybe you feel misunderstood, even by those who know you best. Maybe you've been wrongly accused. Maybe you've been disoriented with the rumors swirling around you. Maybe someday you will feel like you don't have any comrades, any allies, anyone with you or for you at all. Or perhaps you will feel the pain of betrayal by a close friend. But if you are *in* Christ, then you *have* Christ, and he knows you, the real you, the you that others may miss or misunderstand. And because he knows you, *you are Known*—capital *K*, through and through—and *you are accepted*. Jesus "gets" you, and he stands with you through the mistreatment of being misunderstood.

5. Vertical Friendship Transforms Horizontal Friendship

Fifth, friendship with Jesus makes us better friends with others. Vertical friendship empowers horizontal friendship. The greatest power for becoming a better friend is being befriended by the best Friend.

We see this in two ways. First, we always become like our friends; they influence the moral direction of our lives, and the closer the bond, the stronger the influence.

What happens, then, as we grow closer to Christ? We become like him. Which means that we not only experience his constancy, empathy, and so forth—all the things that make him the true and ultimate Friend—but we also begin to reflect these qualities to others. Which means that as we get to know Christ more personally, we become better friends.

As *the* great Friend, Jesus models true friendship; as *our* great Friend, he empowers it.

Second, experiencing fellowship with Jesus frees us to *enjoy* other friends. Jesus fulfills our deepest longings for community so that we don't need to use other people to meet those needs. With Christ as our Friend, we won't turn others into idols. We won't place on them relational expectations that they cannot meet. We won't unload on them relational burdens that they cannot bear. Francis Schaeffer wrote that if someone tries to find everything he needs in a friend, "he destroys the very thing he wants and destroys the one he loves. He sucks them dry, he eats them up, and they, as well as the relationship, are destroyed."[13]

But Christ will never run dry. He is a Niagara of love and grace. Rather than expecting others to fill our cup, we let Christ fill it until it overflows, and then we have something to give everyone else.

6. Missional Friendship

Finally, Jesus invites us to expand his circle of fellowship. He sends us out to welcome others in. In the last chapter, we saw that reconciliation is at the heart of personal salvation. It is also at the heart of the church's mission.

We now even love our enemies with the twofold hope that they would become friends with us and also with Christ. This is a ministry of love. As Martin Luther King Jr. put it, "Love is the only force capable of transforming an enemy into a friend."[14] As those who have received this befriending love, we now extend this to others.

The apostle Paul said that God entrusts us—his enemies turned friends, his reconciled ones—with "the ministry of reconciliation" (2 Cor. 5:18–21). Here's what this means: we not only become friends *with* God, we get to make friends *for* God.

He entrusts us with the ministry of making friends for him. This involves extending God's offer of fellowship through Christ to our neighbors and the nations.

This also means personally befriending those who do not yet know Christ. If you know Jesus, then he commissions you with this ministry of making friends. We befriend others personally, and then we introduce them to the greatest Friend.

And if you don't yet know him in this way, then he opens the invitation to you this very moment.

CONCLUSION

Here's what we've seen: Jesus offers his friendship as a privilege to embrace, a relationship to experience, a covenant to keep, a comfort to receive, a power to tap, and a message to spread.

It's also our only hope in life and death. Friendship with Jesus endures forever—and not because he's "stuck" with us forever but because he wants us forever. Jesus earnestly prayed, "Father, I desire that they also, whom you have given me, may be with me where I am" (John 17:24). Christian, would Jesus miss you if you never joined him in the endless ages to come? The truth is, yes, he would miss you forever. You are his dear friend, closer to his heart than anyone has ever been to yours.

You may lose many friends through the years. But even if every one of them abandons you, Jesus remains. He remains your truest and best Friend. And even as you age and your companions pass away, remember this: "Death may deprive of dear friends, but it can't deprive us of this, our best friend."[15]

And he remains our great Friend even as we approach the end of our own earthly journey. Our great companion will remain with us, at our side, walking with us through death's corridor. In our life, we walk with Jesus one step after another. In our death, we take just one more step with him—a hard step, but one we don't have to take alone.

With that kind of hope for our eternal tomorrow, how then should we live today?

Thomas Goodwin put it best: "You [have] entered into a covenant of friendship with God, make something of it."[16] In other words, as you look to the journey ahead, enjoy the privilege of walking every step, every day, onward into the eternal world of friendship to come.

———

And now may the triune God of communal love
lead us to walk in covenantal friendship with him,
that we might befriend others as he has befriended us.

QUESTIONS FOR REFLECTION AND DISCUSSION

1. To which side of the spectrum do you drift when you think of friendship with Jesus? Do you regard him as so holy that friendship feels unfitting, or do you approach him so casually that friendship seems sentimental? How does the biblical perspective on his friendship balance your understanding?

2. Think about what you know of Jesus's character from the Bible. How does he embody the marks of true friendship? Which characteristic most stands out to you?

3. Charles Spurgeon wrote that it is the solemn duty of Christians to bear witness to the faithfulness of God's friendship. How has God shown himself to be a faithful Friend to you over the past few months or years?

4. At the heart of friendship is conversation. Write down a plan for how you will set aside time each day to listen to God through the Bible and talk to him through prayer. Since the Christian life is walking with the Lord in friendship, how should God's Word and prayer also integrate into the rest of your day?

5. Write down the names of three people in your life who don't know God as their truest Friend. How will you pursue deeper friendship with them? How will you plan to introduce them to your great Friend?

ACKNOWLEDGMENTS

I'm grateful for friends who read and commented on the book: Jon Hoglund, Trent Hunter (my brother who is closer than a brother), Josh and Katie Klos, Dan Montgomery, Johnny Nast, and Taylor Sutton. I'm glad this project gave me an excuse to interact with you about the topic. Your encouragement and insight clarified my thinking and made this book better.

I also think of Bill Chapman, Tim Dyer, Don Jones, Joe Jones, Chris McGarvey, Jonny Miller, Dave Newton, Dave Smith, Jef Spitzler, Wrik Todd, the MEWALO group, fellow leaders and members at Zionsville Fellowship, and other good friends. Thanks to Mom and Dad for raising me to prioritize people and to choose companions wisely. Thanks to the Crossway team, especially Laura Talcott for careful editing and Dave DeWit for steady encouragement and advice.

Thanks to Ray Ortlund Jr. for writing the foreword. You've taught me about the friendly heart of Christ and the gospel culture that flows from knowing him.

In particular, I'm grateful to Dane Ortlund. You encouraged me to write this, you improved my thinking all the way through, and you kept me going through sheer encouragement. I look forward to the new creation when the two of us will enjoy talking with Thomas Goodwin, who has been our companion through his writing, and who has shown us the great heart of our great Friend.

Above all, Christina: Thank you for your covenantal constancy and for happily freeing me up to write. And to our boys—Moses, Isaiah, Chase, and Luke: Because you make life a blast, you helped me write this book in twice the time. I love being your father, and I look forward to growing as friends.

FURTHER READING

Aelred of Rievaulx. *Spiritual Friendship*. Translated by Lawrence C. Braceland. Collegeville, MN: Liturgical Press, 2010.

Aelred was a twelfth-century English monk. Although this is not an easy read, it is one of the few great books on Christian friendship from the past centuries. He affirms the inherent goodness of human friendship by rooting it in God's gift of creation, and he shows how Christian friendship endures forever.

Black, Hugh. *Friendship*. Ontario, Canada: Joshua Press, 2008.

Black was a Scottish pastor and theologian. Writing at the end of the nineteenth century, even then he noted the thinness of the modern view and practice of friendship. He explains the marks and benefits of friendship but also adds insight on how to endure losing friendships through death or relational decay.

Edgar, Brian. *God Is Friendship: A Theology of Spirituality, Community, and Society*. Wilmore, KY: Seedbed Publishing, 2013.

This is a more academic work. Although Edgar does not give much attention to cultivating personal friendships, he shares insights on the topic from historical, theological, and philosophical perspectives. This is the most comprehensive book on friendship from a Christian perspective.

Goodwin, Thomas. "Of Gospel Holiness in Heart and Life," 129–336. Vol. 7 of *The Works of Thomas Goodwin*. Lafayette, IN: Sovereign Grace Publishers, 2001.

Goodwin was an English Puritan pastor and author from the 1600s. His unique gift to us today is his insight into the heart of God. In this stirring work on gospel-centered sanctification, Goodwin frames the whole of the Christian life in terms of friendship with God. This is the best resource available on the neglected topic of friendship with God.

Lewis, C. S. "Friendship," 57–90. In *The Four Loves*. New York: Harcourt and Brace, 1960.

This is an enjoyable and insightful read on the uniqueness of friendship. Lewis explores aspects of friendship that hardly anyone else does, and he explains insights into friendship in a way that only he could.

Roberts, Vaughan. *True Friendship: Walking Shoulder to Shoulder*. Leyland, England: 10Publishing, 2013.

Roberts has a gift of clearly presenting the essential elements of any topic he addresses. *True Friendship* is a concise and practical overview of the central marks of friendship from Proverbs. The best short and practically oriented read on the topic.

Ryle, J. C. "The Best Friend," 317–30. In *Practical Religion*. Carlisle, PA: Banner of Truth, 2013.

This sermon is a sustained exposition of Jesus as our best and greatest Friend. Ryle preached this to commend Jesus as the one true Friend that we all need and want. A delight to read.

Spurgeon, Charles. "The Friends of Jesus." Vol. 26 of *Spurgeon's Sermons: 1880*. Grand Rapids, MI: Christian Classics Ethereal Library. http://www.ccel.org/ccel/spurgeon/sermons26.xli.html.

Spurgeon preached several sermons on the theme of Jesus as our truest Friend. This one, preached from John 15:14, draws attention to Christ's heart of love for his friends and the great honor he gives us when he befriends us.

NOTES

Introduction

1. J. C. Ryle, *Practical Religion* (Carlisle, PA: Banner of Truth, 2013), 317.

Chapter 1: Forgotten Friendship

1. Joseph Epstein, *Friendship: An Exposé* (New York: Houghton Mifflin, 2006), 251.
2. Augustine, Sermon 299D, 1, quoted in A. C. Grayling, *Friendship* (New Haven, CT: Yale University Press, 2013), 66.
3. Jonathan Edwards, *The "Miscellanies": Entry Nos. 1153–1360*, ed. Douglas A. Sweeney, vol. 23 of *The Works of Jonathan Edwards* (New Haven, CT: Yale University Press, 2004), 350.
4. Esther Edwards Burr, *The Journal of Esther Edwards Burr, 1754–1757*, ed. Carol F. Karlsen and Laurie Crumpacker (New Haven, CT: Yale University Press, 1986), 185.
5. Burr, *Journal of Esther Edwards Burr*, 185. I have lightly modernized the language in this and subsequent quotations of Burr.
6. John Newton, *The Letters of John Newton* (Carlisle, PA: Banner of Truth, 2007), 331.
7. Carolinne White, *Christian Friendship in the Fourth Century* (Cambridge: Cambridge University Press, 1992), 69.
8. White, *Christian Friendship in the Fourth Century*, 70.
9. Michael A. van den Berg, *Friends of Calvin* (Grand Rapids, MI: Eerdmans, 2016), viii.
10. John Calvin, *Commentaries on the Epistles to Timothy, Titus, and Philemon*, trans. William Pringle (Grand Rapids, MI: Baker, 2009), 276.
11. Burr, *Journal of Esther Edwards Burr*, 53.
12. Hugh Black, *Friendship* (Ontario, Canada: Joshua Press, 2008), 20.
13. A. C. Grayling, *Friendship* (New Haven, CT: Yale University Press, 2013), 1. Of course, we wonder about marriage and other familial

relationships: Are they not higher and finer than friendship? Grayling anticipates our question and clarifies his point: Parent-child relationships develop into friendships over time, and a marriage is to be the best of friendships. While parenting and marriage are distinct relationships, both ideally grow into deep friendship.

14. Charles Spurgeon, "A Faithful Friend," in *Sermons of Rev. C. H. Spurgeon of London*, vol. 3 (New York: Robert Carter & Brothers, 1883), 11.

15. Proverbs shows, for example, how to find the right kinds of friends (Prov. 13:20; 22:24–25), why to treasure faithful friends (19:6; 27:9–10), and how to avoid the tragedy of separating close friends (16:28; 17:9). It also memorably reminds us, "There is a friend who sticks closer than a brother" (Prov. 18:24).

16. Black, *Friendship*, 19.

17. Aelred of Rievaulx, *Spiritual Friendship*, trans. Lawrence C. Braceland (Collegeville, MN: Liturgical Press, 2010), 106.

18. Janet Kornblum, "Study: 25% of Americans Have No One to Confide In," *USA Today*, June 22, 2006, http://usatoday30.usatoday.com/news/nation/2006-06-22-friendship_x.htm.

19. Another study shows that in 2010, one-third of adults over the age of forty-five reported chronic loneliness. Just ten years earlier, one-fifth of such adults reported the same. G. Oscar Anderson, "Loneliness among Older Adults: A National Survey of Adults 45+," AARP website, September 2010, http://www.aarp.org/research/topics/life/info-2014/loneliness_2010.html.

20. Ceylan Yeginsu, "U.K. Appoints a Minister for Loneliness," *The New York Times*, January 17, 2018, https://www.nytimes.com/2018/01/17/world/europe/uk-britain-loneliness.html.

21. Stephen Marche, "Is Facebook Making Us Lonely?" *The Atlantic*, May 2012, http://www.theatlantic.com/magazine/archive/2012/05/is-facebook-making-us-lonely/308930/.

22. Alexander Nehamas, *On Friendship* (New York: Basic Books, 2016), 31.

23. Epstein, *Friendship*, 62.

24. See Brian Edgar, *God Is Friendship* (Wilmore, KY: Seedbed Publishing, 2013), 88–90.

25. Bronnie Ware, "Regrets of the Dying," *Bronnie Ware* (blog), 2009, http://www.bronnieware.com/blog/regrets-of-the-dying.

26. Ware, "Regrets of the Dying."

Chapter 2: The Edenic Ache

1. Charles Spurgeon, *Sermons of Rev. C. H. Spurgeon of London*, vol. 3 (New York: Robert Carter & Brothers, 1883), 11.

2. Vivek Murthy, "Work and the Loneliness Epidemic," *Harvard Business Review*, September 2017, https://hbr.org/cover-story/2017/09/work-and-the-loneliness-epidemic.

3. Judith Shulevitz, "The Lethality of Loneliness," *New Republic*, May 13, 2013, https://newrepublic.com/article/113176/science-loneliness-how-isolation-can-kill-you.

4. Hugh Black, *Friendship* (Ontario, Canada: Joshua Press, 2008), 19.

5. Martin Luther, *Luther: Letters of Spiritual Counsel*, ed. Theodore G. Tappert (Louisville, KY: Westminster John Knox Press, 2006), 95.

6. Tim Keller, "Spiritual Friendship" (sermon, Redeemer Presbyterian Church, March 1, 1998), http://www.gospelinlife.com/spiritual-friendship-6608.

7. Jason M. Breslow, "What Does Solitary Confinement Do to Your Mind?" *Frontline*, April 22, 2014, http://www.pbs.org/wgbh/frontline/article/what-does-solitary-confinement-do-to-your-mind/.

8. Henry Francis Lyte, "Jesus I My Cross Have Taken" (1825).

9. There are other important ways to answer this question as well. For example, God made us in such a way that his created gifts are a true means of strength and encouragement. With God as our highest joy and deepest source of satisfaction, he nevertheless made us so that we—as creatures—experience renewal through various created means. Food, water, sleep, relationships—all of these bring necessary renewal to our whole, embodied selves. Our physical bodies, our mental faculties, our emotional dispositions—all are interrelated and dependent on God's good, created gifts.

10. John Stott, *The Message of 2 Timothy* (Downers Grove, IL: InterVarsity Press, 1973), 120–21.

11. The question of how we enjoy God's gifts without letting them usurp our highest affection for God is an important one, because at stake is the difference between idolatry and true worship. On navigating this topic, see John Piper, "How to Wield the World in the Fight for Joy" in *When I Don't Desire God* (Wheaton, IL: Crossway, 2004), 175–206.

12. I take the traditional view of this text, which understands the "us" as referring to a divine dialogue within the godhead. The text implies that God is a plurality in unity, which the rest of the Bible affirms and clarifies as a tri-unity. However, many recent Old Testament scholars take "us" to refer to God's speech to a heavenly court of angels about his plans. Neither view is without difficulties, but the traditional view fits best with the immediate and whole-Bible contexts.

13. Donald Macleod, *Shared Life: The Trinity and the Fellowship of God's People* (Fearh, Tain, Scotland: Christian Focus, 2011), 61.

14. Tim Keller, "Spiritual Friendship."
15. Aelred of Rievaulx, *Spiritual Friendship*, trans. by Lawrence C. Braceland (Collegeville, MN: Liturgical Press, 2010), 82.
16. Simon & Garfunkel, "I Am a Rock." Words and music by Paul Simon. Copyright © 1965 Paul Simon. International copyright secured. All rights reserved. I'm thankful to my friend Dan Montgomery for pointing out this song to me.
17. C. S. Lewis, *The Four Loves* (New York: Harcourt & Brace, 1960), 121.

Chapter 3: The Greatest of Worldly Goods
1. C. S. Lewis, *Collected Letters of C. S. Lewis*, ed. Walter Hooper, vol. 2 (New York: HarperCollins, 2004), 174.
2. C. S. Lewis, "The Inner Ring," in *The Weight of Glory* (New York: HarperCollins, 2001), 158.
3. Arthur Brooks, *Gross National Happiness: Why Happiness Matters for America—and How We Can Get More of It* (New York: Basic Books, 2008), 73.
4. C. S. Lewis, *The Four Loves* (New York: Harcourt & Brace, 1960), 72.
5. Martin Luther, *Luther: Letters of Spiritual Counsel*, ed. Theodore G. Tappert (Louisville, KY: Westminster John Knox Press, 2006), 95.
6. "Chester Bennington Last Interview about His Depression Which Caused His Suicide," YouTube website, August 5, 2017, https://www.youtube.com/watch?v=CCpW5g87vHg&feature=youtu.be.
7. John Newton, *Letters by the Rev. John Newton*, ed. Josiah Bull (London: The Religious Tract Society, 1869), 150.
8. Newton, *Letters*, 150.
9. John Bunyan, *The Pilgrim's Progress in Modern English* (Gainesville, FL: Bridge-Logos Publications, 1998), 152.
10. William Cowper, "God Moves in a Mysterious Way" (1774).
11. J. R. R. Tolkien, *The Lord of the Rings* (New York: Houghton Mifflin Harcourt, 2004), 406.
12. Tolkien, *The Lord of the Rings*, 406.
13. J. R. R. Tolkien, *The Letters of J. R. R. Tolkien*, ed. Humphrey Carpenter (New York: Houghton Mifflin Harcourt, 2000), 362.
14. Lewis, *The Four Loves*, 80.
15. P. G. Wodehouse, *Carry On, Jeeves* (New York: Overlook Press, 2003), 149.
16. Sesame Street, "What Is a Friend?" YouTube video, February 24, 2012, https://www.youtube.com/watch?v=iPux6QAkBdc.

17. A. C. Grayling, *Friendship* (New Haven, CT: Yale University Press, 2013), 178–79.

Chapter 4: A Friend Who Is as Your Own Soul

1. John Chrysostom, *Homilies on the Epistles to the Galatians, Ephesians, Philippians, Colossians, Thessalonians, Timothy, Titus, and Philemon*, vol. 8 of *Nicene and Post-Nicene Fathers*, ed. Philip Schaff (Peabody, MA: Hendrickson Publishers, 1994), 331.

2. Proverbs 2:17 refers to a spouse as an *alluph*, the strongest word for friend in the Old Testament. In Song of Solomon 5:16, the woman says, "This is my beloved and this is my friend."

3. This phrase is often translated "your closest friend." It is found in only three other places in the Old Testament, two of which refer to David and Jonathan's friendship (1 Sam 18:1, 3; cf. Deut. 13:6). The New Testament sometimes refers to friendship with an equally intriguing word: *idios*, or, "one's own." The apostle Paul's friends are his own (Acts 24:23). This identifies a friend with oneself.

4. This is similar to Aristotle's definition of friendship as "a single soul dwelling in two bodies."

5. Mark Smith, *Tolkien's Ordinary Virtues: Exploring the Spiritual Themes of Lord of the Rings* (Downers Grove, IL: InterVarsity Press, 2002), 26.

6. C. S. Lewis, *The Four Loves* (New York: Harcourt & Brace, 1960), 72.

7. This idiom is charged with emotion. In his study on friendship, Saul Oylan notes that the only other place in the Old Testament where it is used is Genesis 44:30–31, where it describes Jacob's love for his son as "a love so intense that the son's demise would result in the death of the father." Saul Oylan, *Friendship in the Hebrew Bible* (New Haven, CT: Yale University Press, 2017), 110.

8. Lewis, *The Four Loves*, 63. Toward an explanation, our modern culture's view of gender and sexuality have both shifted. First, we now view masculinity as less emotional and more aggressive. Second, although we understand someone who has lust without love, we can no longer understand someone having affectionate love without lust. In light of these shifts, expressions of affection among men immediately seem nonmasculine or sexual. To consider how shifts in a culture's understanding of gender and sexuality affect our practice of friendship, see Richard Godbeer, *The Overflowing of Friendship: Love Between Men and the Creation of the American Republic* (Baltimore, MD: Johns Hopkins University Press, 2009), 73–74, 86, 195–96; and Anthony Esolen, "A Requiem for Friendship: Why Boys Will Not Be Boys & Other Consequences of the Sexual Revolution," *Touchstone*

18, no. 7 (September 2005): 21, http://www.touchstonemag.com/archives/article.php?id=18-07-021-f.

9. Peter Leithart, *A Son to Me* (Moscow, ID: Canon Press, 2003), 110.

10. P. G. Wodehouse, *The Code of the Woosters* (New York: Norton, 2011), 224.

11. Aelred of Rievaulx, *Spiritual Friendship*, trans. by Lawrence C. Braceland (Collegeville, MN: Liturgical Press, 2010), 90. Similarly, Jeremy Taylor wrote that once a friendship is rooted and established, "treat thy friend nobly, love to be with him, do to him all the worthiness of love and fair endearment . . . bear with his infirmities till they approach towards being criminal . . . but never despise him, never leave him." Jeremy Taylor, *A Discourse of the Nature, Offices, and Measures of Friendship*, in vol. 3 of *The Whole Works of the Right Rev. Jeremy Taylor* (London: Frederick Westley & A. H. Davis, 1835), 44.

12. Thomas Goodwin, *The Works of Thomas Goodwin*, vol. 7 (Lafayette, IN: Sovereign Grace Publishers, 2001), 220.

13. Charles Spurgeon, "The Best Friend," in *Spurgeon's Sermons: 1899*, vol. 45 (Grand Rapids, MI: Christian Classics Ethereal Library), https://www.ccel.org/ccel/spurgeon/sermons45.xxv.html.

14. Lewis, *The Four Loves*, 66.

15. Thomas Brooks, *Smooth Stones Taken from Ancient Brooks*, ed. Charles Spurgeon (Carlisle, PA: Banner of Truth, 2011), 137. I have slightly modernized the English.

16. Lewis, *The Four Loves*, 71.

Chapter 5: Cultivating Friendship

1. C. S. Lewis, *Collected Letters of C. S. Lewis*, ed. Walter Hooper, vol. 2 (New York: HarperCollins, 2004), 174.

2. Joseph Epstein, *Friendship: An Exposé* (New York: Houghton Mifflin, 2006), 243.

3. Esther Edwards Burr, *The Journal of Esther Edwards Burr, 1754–1757*, ed. Carol F. Karlsen and Laurie Crumpacker (New Haven, CT: Yale University Press, 1986), 50.

4. Aelred of Rievaulx, *Spiritual Friendship*, trans. by Lawrence C. Braceland (Collegeville, MN: Liturgical Press, 2010), 100.

5. Thomas Goodwin, *The Works of Thomas Goodwin*, vol. 7 (Lafayette, IN: Sovereign Grace Publishers, 2001), 197–98. I've updated the English slightly.

6. Quoted in Michael A. van den Berg, *Friends of Calvin* (Grand Rapids, MI: Eerdmans, 2016), 115.

7. LICC media, "John Stott on 'When I Feel Most Alive,'" YouTube video, August 6, 2010, https://www.youtube.com/watch?v=MDPqw-LAuaU.

8. Ronald L. Giese Jr., "'Iron Sharpens Iron' as a Negative Image: Challenging the Common Interpretation of Proverbs 27:17," *Journal of Biblical Literature* 135, no. 1 (2016): 76 [61–76].

9. Burr, *Journal of Esther Edwards Burr*, 50.

Chapter 6: A Biblical Theology of Friendship

1. Charles Spurgeon, "The Friends of Jesus," in *Spurgeon's Sermons: 1880*, vol. 26 (Grand Rapids, MI: Christian Classics Ethereal Library), http://www.ccel.org/ccel/spurgeon/sermons26.xli.html.

2. Richard Sibbes wrote, "The Father, Son, and Holy [Spirit] were happy in themselves, and enjoyed one another before the world was. But that God delights to communicate and spread his goodness, there had never been a creation nor a redemption." Richard Sibbes, "The Successful Seeker," in *Works of Richard Sibbes*, vol. 6 (Edinburgh: James Nichol, 1862–64), 113, quoted in R. N. Frost, *Richard Sibbes: God's Spreading Goodness* (Vancouver, WA: Cor Deo Press, 2012), 102.

3. Kevin Vanhoozer, *Remythologizing Theology* (New York: Cambridge University Press, 2010), 259.

4. See G. K. Beale, *The Temple and the Church's Mission: A Biblical Theology of the Dwelling Place of God* (Downers Grove, IL: IVP Academic, 2004), 66, 111; and Gordon Wenham, *Genesis 1–15*, vol. 1 (Grand Rapids, MI: Zondervan, 2014), 76, 90.

5. See also Deuteronomy 23:14; 2 Samuel 7:6–7.

6. Proverbs 13:20 says, "Whoever walks with the wise becomes wise, but the companion of fools will suffer harm." Here, "walks with" is in parallel with "the companion," a common translation of a Hebrew word for friend. See also Proverbs 1:15; Job 34:8; Amos 3:3; Hosea 11:12; Micah 6:8; Malachi 2:6.

7. Thomas Goodwin, *The Works of Thomas Goodwin*, vol. 7 (Lafayette, IN: Sovereign Grace Publishers, 2001), 204.

8. And God made the final covenant in the Old Testament, the Davidic covenant, with David, a man who related to him on particularly intimate terms.

9. For example, Psalm 25:14 says that God's "secrets" or "counsel" is for those who fear him (see also Prov. 3:32; Job 29:4). Those who trusted God within the old covenant experienced his counsel.

10. Craig Keener, *The Gospel of John: A Commentary*, vol. 2 (Peabody, MA: Hendrickson, 2003), 1014. In other words, as many commentators

on the Gospel of John note, this is not merely referring to a transition in the lives of the disciples, but a transition in redemptive history.

11. Jonathan Edwards, "197. Rev. 17:14," in *Sermons, Series II, 1731–1732*, ed. Jonathan Edwards Center, vol. 46 (WJE Online). I've updated the grammar.

12. Richard Bauckham, *The Gospel of Glory: Major Themes in Johannine Theology* (Grand Rapids, MI: Baker Academic, 2015), 69.

13. Bauckham, *Gospel of Glory*, 69.

14. John Stott, *The Cross of Christ* (Downers Grove, IL: InterVarsity Press, 1986), 192.

15. Walter Marshall, *The Gospel Mystery of Sanctification: Growing in Holiness by Living in Union with Christ*, ed. Bruce H. McRae (Eugene, OR: Wipf & Stock, 2005), 261.

16. On the widespread use of these two phrases in Greek thought, see Carolinne White, *Christian Friendship in the Fourth Century* (Cambridge: Cambridge University Press, 1992), 44; and Brian Edgar, *God Is Friendship* (Wilmore, KY: Seedbed Publishing, 2013), 141.

17. Gordon Fee, *Paul's Letter to the Philippians* (Grand Rapids, MI: Eerdmans, 1995), 12.

18. Fee, *Paul's Letter to the Philippians*, 13.

Chapter 7: The Great Friend

1. James Strahan, "The Perfect Friendship," *The Expository Times*, November 1, 1911.

2. Charles Spurgeon, "Friendship's Guide," in *Spurgeon's Sermons: 1914*, vol. 60 (Grand Rapids, MI: Christian Classics Ethereal Library), https://www.ccel.org/ccel/spurgeon/sermons60.li.html.

3. Charles Spurgeon, "A Faithful Friend," in *Sermons of C. H. Spurgeon* (New York: Sheldon, Blakeman & Co., 1857), 13–14. I've slightly modified the wording here.

4. Thomas Goodwin, *The Works of Thomas Goodwin*, vol. 7 (Lafayette, IN: Sovereign Grace Publishers, 2001), 192.

5. There are other reasons for Jesus's great emotion here: He is angered at death. He is deeply moved and troubled because he knew that when he raised Lazarus as the greatest "sign" of his ministry, it would be the decisive act that settled the Jewish leaders in their decision to kill him. By raising Lazarus, Jesus tips the decisive domino that will lead to his own death. Jesus is, in effect, laying his own life down for his friend. See also Richard Bauckham's observations in *The Gospel of Glory: Major Themes in Johannine Theology* (Grand Rapids, MI: Baker Academic, 2015), 66–67.

6. A man named Nathan Cole, describing his experience when listening to George Whitefield preach. Quoted in Arnold Dallimore, *George Whitefield: The Life and Times of the Great Evangelist of the Eighteenth-Century Revival*, vol. 1 (London: Banner of Truth, 1970), 541.

7. Jonathan Edwards, "The Excellency of Christ," in *Sermons and Discourses, 1734–1738*, ed. M. X. Lesser, vol. 19 in *The Works of Jonathan Edwards* (New Haven, CT: Yale University Press, 2001), 588. This is one of Edwards's most famous sermons, and it is largely about friendship, especially friendship with Christ.

8. J. I. Packer, *Knowing God* (Downers Grove, IL: InterVarsity Press, 1973), 42.

9. Jonathan Edwards, *The "Miscellanies": Entry Nos. 1153–1360*, ed. Douglas A. Sweeney, vol. 23 of *The Works of Jonathan Edwards* (New Haven, CT: Yale University Press, 2004), 350.

10. Charles Spurgeon, *All of Grace* (Grand Rapids, MI: Christian Classics Ethereal Library), https://www.ccel.org/ccel/spurgeon/grace/files/grace .html.

11. J. C. Ryle, *Expository Thoughts on the Gospels*, *St. John*, vol. 3 (London: William Hunt, 1873), 128.

12. John Paton, *John G. Paton: Missionary to the New Hebrides*, ed. James Paton (Carlisle, PA: Banner of Truth, 2007), 200.

13. Francis Schaeffer, *True Spirituality* (Carol Stream, IL: Tyndale, 2001), 142.

14. Martin Luther King Jr., *Strength to Love* (Minneapolis: Fortress Press, 2010), 48.

15. Jonathan Edwards, "136. To Lady Mary Pepperrell," in *Letters and Personal Writings*, ed. George S. Claghorn, vol. 16 of *The Works of Jonathan Edwards* (New Haven, CT: Yale University Press, 1998), 418.

16. Goodwin, *Works of Thomas Goodwin*, 190.

GENERAL INDEX

Abraham, 127–29, 152
acquaintanceship, 28–29, 78, 95, 100–1
Adam, 42–46, 48, 53, 108, 124–29
Aelred of Rievaulx, 24, 49, 84, 161, 170n11
affection
  in friendship, 62–63, 66, 73, 80–84, 91, 110, 169n8
  with God, 130, 167n11
  of Jesus, 142–43, 148, 152
agape (love), 34–35
Allah, 48
anxiety, 43, 66, 88
Aristotle, 22, 169n4
Augustine, 20, 39

Basil the Great, 21
Bauckham, Richard, 131, 172n5
Beecher, Henry Ward, 75
Bennington, Chester, 65
Bible reading, 46, 67, 89, 105, 109, 146, 150–51
Black, Hugh, 22, 23, 97
Brooks, Thomas, 92
Bunyan, John, 67–68
Burr, Aaron, 20

Burr, Esther Edwards, 20–22, 101, 165n5
busyness, 30–31, 34, 38, 99

Calvin, John, 21, 103
candor, 87, 127, 147–48
Christ. *See* Jesus Christ
Christianity
  is friendship with God, 23, 140, 158, 162
Chrysostom, John, 77
church
  diversity in the, 92–93, 135
  friendship in the, 28, 34, 52, 92–93, 110, 134–36, 138, 149–50, 155
  mission of the, 128, 136, 155–56
communion
  in friendship, 31–32, 103
  with God, 149–50
  the Lord's Supper, 150
  in the Trinity, 122, 124
community, 34, 42, 45, 50, 107, 134–36, 155, 161
conversation
  with friends, 46, 52–55, 60, 62, 68, 88, 102–5, 110–11, 150, 158

175

SCRIPTURE INDEX